DELIGHTS
OF
SCANDINAVIAN
COOKING

DELIGHTS
OF
SCANDINAVIAN
COOKING

With 113 traditional recipes
adapted by Renate Kissel
and photographed exclusively
for this book by
Hans Joachim Döbbelin

ANGLO-NORDIC
IMPRINTS

Illustration on page 2:
Scandinavia – Land of the Midnight Sun, of endless forests and thousands of lakes. The landscape ranges from the gentle plains of Denmark to Sweden's host of picturesque rocky islands; from the shimmering lakelands of Finland to the jagged cliffs of the west coast of Norway. The Nærøyfjord, one of the most beautiful of all the Norwegian fjords, is just one example of the magnificent scenery.

© 1990 Sigloch Edition, Zeppelinstraße 35a, D-7118 Künzelsau
Sigloch Edition & Co., Lettenstrasse 3, CH-6343 Rotkreuz
This edition published by arrangement with Sigloch Edition
for Anglo-Nordic Imprints Ltd., 15 Marshall Road, Godalming, Surrey GU7 3AS, England
Copying prohibited. All rights reserved. Printed in Germany
Translation: Pholiota Translations, London
Colour processing: PHG Lithos, Martinsried
Typesetting: Setzerei Lihs, Ludwigsburg
Printing: Erasmusdruck, Mainz
Paper: 135 g/m² BVS made by Papierfabrik Scheufelen, Lenningen
Binding: Sigloch Buchbinderei, Künzelsau
ISBN 1-873581-15-7

In the Land of the Midnight Sun

Imagine sitting by an open log fire outside a lonely cottage deep in the Scandinavian countryside, in one of the vast forests of the North, or beside a quiet lake. As you grill the fish you have just caught over the fire, you have plenty of time to enjoy the magnificent spectacle of the sun slowly setting over the water. At these latitudes the sun is in no hurry to set.

As you get to know the Scandinavians, you will discover how deeply-rooted the ancient traditions and customs still are. This is par-ticularly evident in Scandinavian cooking. Scandinavian cuisine has always been based on local produce. Much use is made of wild foods, particularly game – elk, reindeer, snow hare and snow grouse. The abundance of seafood and fish – salmon, herring, trout, lobster, oysters, mussels and crayfish – is put to good use at the Nordic table. Scandinavian cuisine can be described as plain, hearty fare, and of the finest quality.

A culinary journey through Scandinavia becomes a special voyage of discovery.

*The Scandinavians have a very close and pro-
found relationship with nature and are happy
to enjoy what the countryside provides. In the
autumn, they love to roam the woods collecting wild mushrooms and berries. Lingonberries (left) are especially popular. They are
served fresh with roast game, and they are
also used to make delicious desserts and
liqueurs.*

Food from the Sea, Forest and Field

The peoples of the far north have always had to struggle to find food to an extent unknown in more southerly latitudes. The grain crop hardly has time to ripen during the Scandinavian summer, especially if the sun does not shine often enough. This means that the wheat grains need to be dried out artificially – an expensive process – and milled quickly. Bread keeps best if it is made from wholemeal rather than refined white flour, so there are many different kinds of wholemeal bread in Scandinavia. Many of these are crispbreads, which keep especially well.

Scandinavians like to accompany their game dishes with the fruits of the forest, wild berries and mushrooms. Lingonberries, for instance, are served with roast meat. Lingonberries are similar to cranberries but have a more delicate, resinous flavour. They can be preserved merely by storing in cold water because their high acidity is a good preservative. Lingonberries are eaten with savoury roasts, and they also taste excellent with barley, rye or oatmeal porridge and, of course, in puddings.

The cloudberry, which the Finns call *lakka*, grows in the far north. It is a golden-yellow fruit which resembles the raspberry or blackberry in appearance, and has a high vitamin C content. It is used to make the famous cloudberry liqueur. The Arctic raspberry, known in Finnish as *mesimarja*, is used to make another well-known liqueur.

As long ago as Viking times, chicken, duck or goose were very popular and they remain so today. A traditional way of serving goose is to salt it down. It is known in Norway as *Spengt Gås*, in Sweden as *Språngd Gås* and in Denmark as *Sprængd Gås*. The goose is soaked in brine for several days in order to make its flesh especially soft and tender. Duck, prepared in the same way, is popular in Denmark.

Pork and beef are the main meats eaten in Scandinavia, but lamb is also popular. Lamb and cabbage stew is a warming winter dish and roast leg of lamb is the centrepiece of the classic Easter Sunday dinner. In Norway, many farmhouses still have turf roofs on which goats happily graze in the summer months. They provide the milk for *geitost*, the savoury goat's cheese resembling a block of smooth peanut butter which provides a delicious ending to a typical Norwegian meal.

A variety of cultured milks, fresh and sour cream and salted butter have been staple ingredients of the Scandinavian diet for more than a thousand years. These dairy products added variety and extended the use of fresh milk, which is still the most popular drink with meals throughout the Nordic countries.

The crowning glory of the Scandinavian diet is the harvest of the sea and lakes. The Vikings, who mainly inhabited the coastal areas, appreciated oysters, mussels, crayfish, herring, mackerel, salmon and trout. Whalemeat was also a traditional food. In Norway, whalemeat is roasted or smoked like ham and is considered a great delicacy.

Herring is definitely the prime fish of Scandinavia. There are so many ways to prepare and serve it, that it is hard to imagine what the famous Scandinavian buffets – such as the Danish *smørrebrød*, the Swedish *smörgåsbord*, the Norwegian *koldbord* and the Finnish *voileipäpöytä* – would be like without it. There are two distinct varieties, the Atlantic herring and the smaller more delicate Baltic herring often called "the poor man's salmon". Salmon is a special delicacy. It is prepared in many ways – poached, grilled, fried or smoked. Salt-cured salmon, once confined to Scandinavia, has now become fashionable throughout Europe. The Swedes call it *gravad lax*. The fish is cured in its raw state and is ready to eat after two or three days' salting. It is served with a sweet mustard sauce. As in so many Scandinavian dishes, an abundance of fresh dill is used in the preserving process. This herb flourishes in every garden in the northern latitudes; its flavour, and that of horseradish, are a distinctive feature of Nordic cuisine.

The start of the crayfish season towards the end of July is a cause for real celebration in Sweden and Finland. Families and friends get together in their lakeside cabins to enjoy this special delicacy. Freshwater crayfish can only flourish in the cleanest rivers and lakes. They are caught at night using special nets.

Preparations for a crayfish party start the night before, when the crayfish are boiled in huge pots of water flavoured with salt and dill. They are left to cool in the water to absorb the flavours. For the party itself, wooden tables are laid out in the open and before the feasting begins, appetites are sharpened by a visit to the sauna or a swim in the lake. The crayfish are served in a large basket or tray decorated with bunches of fresh dill. Colourful paper tablecloths, bundles of napkins – and even bibs – together with paper lanterns and candles all reflect the red of the crayfish.

The only other requirement is a crayfish knife, which has a strong, short, pointed blade with a hole in it. This is used for removing the tips of the claws so that they are easier to crack. As much of the white claw-meat as possible is extracted and then the rest is sucked out. The tail is detached from the body and the tail-flesh is removed from its shell in one piece. After removing the dark vein, the delicate white meat is sprinkled with chopped dill and eaten with lots of buttered toast. The custom is to place the empty shells around the rim of the plate, heads pointing outwards.

Akvavit (Snaps), a clear spirit flavoured with caraway seed, vodka or ice-cold beer accompanies the crustaceans. The custom is to drink a small glass of spirits, eat a crayfish, drink another glass, eat another crayfish and so on, thus guaranteeing a merry evening!

The art of brewing dates back to Viking times. It used to be one of the most important duties of a Viking wife. Nowadays, all the Nordic countries brew good beer from the finest natural ingredients. For the Danes, beer is something of a national drink, and they have popularised their native lagers throughout the world. Norway's and Sweden's liquor laws have turned low-alcohol beer into a popular drink. Akvavit or Snaps is the favourite spirit in most of Scandinavia, though the Finns prefer vodka.

Akvavit is drunk as an apéritif and is said to be an aid to the digestion. It is made in a wide range of flavours, including vermouth, anise, pepper and mixed herbs, in addition to the traditional caraway. Linie-akvavit, made in Norway, has an interesting history. It used to be stored in oak barrels as part of a ship's provisions and taken on long voyages, which involved crossing the equator. The constant rocking motion of the ship and the fluctuations in temperature was found to improve the quality and make the drink more mellow. This method became part of the production process and is still in use today. Linie-Akvavit is bottled upon the ship's return and labelled with the name of the ship and the dates of the voyage. Akvavit should always be served ice-cold.

A Scandinavian meal often ends with coffee and cake or pastries. As in olden times, coffee is brought to the boil on the stove in an old-fashioned coffee pot, not brewed in hot water as in the rest of Europe. The Scandinavians are real world champions at coffee consumption!

Coffee tastes best when you have something to eat with it. The Danes drink their coffee with the delicious pastries for which they are world-famous and which in Denmark are somehow lighter and flakier than when made anywhere else. At a Swedish birthday party there are always at least seven different kinds of cake or biscuit on the table.

Hard Bread and Salted Fish

Modern Scandinavian cuisine owes much to the eating traditions of the past. When the short summer and the ripening period were over, the most important consideration was to ensure that the harvest would keep well. The resourceful Vikings invented many original methods of food conservation. Bread was baked in such a way as to ensure that most of the moisture evaporated. This made it crisp and hard, so that it would keep fresh for months on end. The bread was then stacked in storehouses. In Finland, the bread was made with a hole in the centre, so the rounds could be threaded on to a rod which was hung from the rafters. This kind of crispbread is still very popular.

Every kind of food needed to be preserved if people were to survive the long, hard winters. A variety of methods was used, including drying. To dry fish, these simple methods are still used. The gutted fish, usually North Atlantic cod, are tied together by the tail in pairs and hung up to dry, unsalted, on wooden racks. The wind gradually evaporates the moisture and the result is called *stokkfisk* (stockfish). *Klippfisk* (literally "cliff-fish") is a Norwegian speciality for which the fish is split in half, then boned and salted and laid out to dry on the high, exposed cliffs overlooking the sea and the fjords. These were the staple provisions which the Vikings took with them on their long sea voyages. The fish were not only eaten at sea but became an ideal item for barter. That is how stockfish reached Spain and Portugal where it still features on the menu as *bacalà* or *bacala*. In Norway, these dried fish are known as *tørrfisk* and are still popular despite the ready availability of fresh cod.

Another method used to preserve food in the past was curing. Fish and meat preserved in salt are still popular today. A good example is the popular Swedish delicacy, *gravad lax*.

Curing requires a great deal of salt. As the Baltic and North Seas have quite a low salt content, the vital need for large quantities of salt generated a brisk trade with southern Europe. This was one of the principal ways in which the Hanseatic League attained such great wealth. Trading posts were set up in strategic ports, such as Bergen in Norway and Visby in Gotland. These cities are still important centres of trade.

Salt was so scarce and expensive for the common people that they were forced to find other methods of food preservation. Fish and meat were simply covered in whey, a method used by the Vikings. Another method – though one which does not preserve it in the fresh state – is to bury fish in the earth for some time. In northern Sweden, Baltic herring is treated in this way. After a time the soil gives it a characteristic and unique flavour and smell, which is something of an acquired taste. The result is known as *surströmming*.

The Scandinavians still use traditional methods to preserve their food.

To make stockfish (above), as soon as the boat has docked, the fish are carefully gutted, tied together by the tail in pairs and hung over a wooden rack in the open air. The brisk Atlantic wind evaporates most of the moisture leaving them as stiff as a board. Stockfish keep for a considerable length of time and are easy to store. This was a real asset to the Vikings when they set sail on their long voyages.

Crispbreads and flatbreads are lighter and keep longer than risen breads. There are just as many kinds of crispbread as ordinary bread in Scandinavia (right). The hole in the middle of the round crispbread is a relic of the days when the best way to preserve it was to thread it on a rod and store it in the rafters.

Same (Lapps) in their traditional dress. No-one really knows where this mysterious people came from. They once populated large parts of Scandinavia, but today their numbers have dwindled to about forty thousand. These semi-nomads were pushed northwards and many were assimilated into the surrounding population. For hundreds of years, the Same have wandered across national borders over the area known as Lapland, grazing their reindeer herds from the summer grasslands on the coast to the highlands of the Finn-markskvidda, where they spend the winter. Today, only about eight hundred families live entirely by herding reindeer.

Scandinavia – A Variety of Cultures

The Scandinavian nations have much in common. Their shared traditions, customs and cuisine can be traced back to the Vikings. The Finns have a slightly different history. This is reflected in the Finnish language, which is not related to the other Nordic languages. The Finns moved northwards, about 1,800 years ago, to the land which they now call home. It was not until they were conquered by the Swedes, who ruled Finland as part of Sweden from the 12th to the 19th centuries, that they absorbed some Nordic influence. Their eating habits and traditions also reflect some Russian influence.

When speaking of Scandinavian people, the *Same* should be mentioned. In English, they are more commonly known as Lapps, though it is a name they do not particularly care for. The *Same* population numbers only about forty thousand. At one time they occupied a large part of Finland before they were gradually pushed northwards. Today they live as nomads, tending their reindeer herds north of the Arctic Circle in the area known as Lapland, which extends across Norway, Sweden, Denmark, Finland and into Russia.

The Scandinavian kitchen varies according to the countryside from which it draws its ingredients. Both Denmark and southern Sweden have fertile agricultural land which provides ample grain harvests. The food in this part of the world is therefore rich and abundant. People of the southern Swedish province of Skåne, with its flat landscape of wheat and rye fields, have the reputation of being well-fed and jolly.

Norway, on the other hand, is criss-crossed with rugged mountain ranges, making farming more difficult. From early times, the Norwegians have had to find much of their food in the sea, so fish is a staple of the Norwegian diet.

The forests, lakes and tundra of central and northern Sweden are not only beautiful but yield a plentiful supply of berries, wild mushrooms and freshwater fish. These foods have an important place in the local cuisine.

Finland is the land of a hundred thousand lakes and vast forests. It has a distinctive cooking style, consisting of nourishing plain fare. There is much Russian influence noticeable in the piirakkas and blinis.

Iceland and Greenland are also part of Scandinavia. Iceland was first inhabited in 874, and was one of the earliest parliamentary democracies. In the 12th century, the island was claimed by Norway, but in 1380 Norway, and consequently Iceland, fell under Danish rule. Iceland only gained complete independence in 1944. Greenland was similarly first Norwegian then Danish, and seceded from Denmark in 1979.

One thing that all Scandinavians have in common is their true artistry in creating and preparing dishes. Every housewife has her secret recipes. Elegant and distinctive cutlery and china with fresh flowers and candles grace the table at family meals. For Scandinavians the enjoyment of good food in good company is an important part of their way of life.

Denmark consists of a patchwork of islands, surrounding the mainland peninsula. In addition to the 18 Faroe Islands in the North Atlantic, the kingdom of Denmark consists of more than 400 larger and smaller islands. About 100 of these are inhabited. The small ferry port of Mommark (above) lies in the southeastern corner of the Jutland Peninsula which links Denmark to the European mainland.

A Land Flowing with Milk and Honey

Denmark, surrounded by the North Sea, the Skagerrak and the Kattegat channels, links Central Europe with Scandinavia. It consists of the Jutland Peninsula plus over 400 islands, of which only about 100 are inhabited. The mainland landscape is flat or undulating, and the highest point is only 173 metres (about 550 feet). The scenery is nevertheless very varied. There is marshland in the south, wooded hills in the interior, and moorland, lakes and fertile farmland. There are no major rivers in Denmark, only lakes, pools and wetlands. The Danish islands are full of contrasts. Like the rest of Denmark, they tend to be flatter and greener than the other Scandinavian islands, which are hilly and rugged. The island of Møn has steep chalk cliffs. Denmark has long stretches of flat, white, sandy beaches. The fjords extend far inland. In stark contrast to Norway, where these arms of the sea are bordered by steeply sloping mountainsides and cliffs, in Denmark they cut deep into the flatlands.

Each of Denmark's main islands has its own individual character. Zealand contains the Copenhagen metropolis – København (Copenhagen) "the trading port" in Danish. It is a majestic island, redolent with history, and undoubtedly the heart of Denmark. Copenhagen was founded in 1167. It has many bridges, splendid castles, copper roofs with their patina of verdigris, a famous harbour and the statue of the Little Mermaid. Copenhagen has much to offer in the way of entertainment, including art and culture. In the centre of the throbbing city, the famous Tivoli Gardens amusement park is a fairy-tale world of coloured lanterns, banks of flowers, fountains, elegant restaurants and concert halls. The city also has a bustling commercial centre. The shopping centre in the old town, the longest pedestrian precinct in the world, is a popular meeting-place. There are countless restaurants and even more *smørrebrød* shops,

cosy street cafés and cakeshops. This shoppers' paradise is bounded by the Town Hall, the Royal New Market and the Round Tower on the Strøget. This is the place to experience the Danish weakness for good food!

Fyn was the island home of the writer of fairytales, Hans Christian Andersen. The Little Mermaid in Copenhagen is a character from one of his most beautiful stories. Fyn is often referred to as the granary of Denmark, and the numerous stately manor houses and castles are proof of this wealth. Delightful old towns and fishing villages are scattered among rolling grasslands and the patchwork of fields.

Lolland and Falster are Denmark's orchards. Their cliffs and beaches are a source of amber, a product of nature up to sixty million years old. The yellow or brown, sometimes even blueish, amber is made into jewellery. This ancient handicraft dates back well over one thousand years.

The neighbouring island of Møn features several dolmens, stone burial vaults, long barrows and other monuments from the early Stone Age. The fact that here, as in the rest of the country, these prehistoric graves have remained intact to the present day shows the respect the Danes have for their heritage. The 12th- and 13th-century white or terracottacoloured village churches are also an outstanding feature of the Møn landscape. They are decorated on the outside with frescoes illustrating scenes from the Bible and testify to the Danes' early talent for artistic design.

The Danish holiday island of Bornholm lies 150 km (88 miles) east of the mainland. For many centuries it was a bulwark against invasion from the East. Its colourful diversity is a microcosm of the Danish landscape, with its golden fields of rapeseed, prosperous farms, forests and thousand-year-old round white churches. The churches here were well-fortified to afford the natives protection from enemy attack. There are manorial estates and old village inns, the popular *kroer*. Entering a *kro* is like stepping into the past. The tradition of a cosy welcoming atmosphere and good food is very much alive here.

The eighteen Faroe Islands, famous for their knitted sweaters, are very tradition-conscious and belong to Denmark. Fish is the staple of the diet and the most important export.

Although Greenland is no longer Danish, Denmark is the island's biggest trading partner. The main Greenland exports are lamb, ewe's milk cheese and, of course, fish.

The Danes left their mark on the rest of the world very early on in their history. In the 6th century, the Norsemen who came down from the far north, and were later called Vikings, gradually began to colonise southern Sweden and Denmark. The Angles, Saxons, Jutes and Huns, who had settled there previously, migrated southwards. The Vikings were good administrators and rulers. The runestones are the earliest written records of their deeds. In 950 A.D., one such runestone was erected by King Harald Bluetooth in Jelling on Jutland. It records the unification of Denmark, the acquisition of Norway and the conversion of the country to Christianity. Runestones are to be found way beyond the shores of Scandinavia, in fact wherever Vikings travelled and brought scribes to record their deeds.

The Vikings were outstanding seafarers, expert in the art of shipbuilding and navigation. Examples of their ships have survived and can be admired today in such places as Roskilde on Zealand and just outside Oslo, where the Oseberg burial ship is on display. The Roman historian Tacitus mentions their streamlined boats in the accounts of his travels. They were faster and had greater manoeuverability than those of their opponents. This was a crucial advantage on their long voyages of discovery and for conducting successful raiding parties. The Vikings occupied large parts of England and Ireland but their urge to travel far afield carried them way down the coast of Europe, past France. In

Normandy, whose name means "Land of the Norsemen", they established a dukedom and they settled in Sicily and Apulia where they amassed tremendous wealth. Their travels took them as far as the Black Sea. Erik the Red sailed from Iceland to Greenland and Leif Erikson discovered America in 1000 A.D. But the true home of the Vikings remained Denmark. Powerful Denmark occasionally united with other Scandinavian countries. There was a union with Sweden until the beginning of the 16th century and with Norway until as recently as 1814. From the daring Vikings, once dreaded throughout Europe, the Danes have evolved into a peace-loving and cultured people. Danes are famous for their tolerance and natural self-confidence.

A traveller to Denmark today is impressed by the Danish appreciation of beautiful design, both in the stylishly-built houses and the elegant household furnishings and tableware. Royal Copenhagen porcelain is just one example of world-famous Danish design.

A lover of good food will greatly enjoy a trip to Denmark. Eating is such an important preoccupation in this country that three meals a day are just not enough. Danes love to find excuses for two or three extra meal breaks and snacks, perhaps just to enjoy a delicious Danish pastry made from *wienerbrødsdej*, a yeast puff pastry dough filled with nuts, marzipan, vanilla or chocolate pastry cream and dusted with sugar. The pastries are usually enjoyed with one or more cups of coffee.

Another snack temptation is the delicious *smørrebrød*, which when translated literally simply means "buttered bread", but this is something of an understatement. *Smørrebrød*, the Danish open sandwich, is so lavish that it is often a complete meal in itself.

Basically, Danish eating habits derive from two traditions, the courtly cuisine of the nobility and the homely food of the peasants. The aristocracy and its food was heavily influenced by foreign customs, especially French cuisine. The dishes sometimes became exaggeratedly refined, so simple country fare was a welcome balancing influence. As a result, Danish cooking is very varied.

The Danes are big producers of pork and eat more of it than the other Scandinavians. Hams are smoked and salted and there is bacon, roast pork, brawn and sausages. Loin of pork with sour apples and potatoes is a classic dish. They are also Scandinavia's biggest meat-eaters. Meat is expensive, so the resourceful Danish housewife has made a virtue out of necessity and invented ways to make it go further. This has produced delicious dishes such as the Danish *frikadeller* – rissoles. Frikadeller are made with ground pork, beef or lamb.

Game is also popular. In Denmark, local game is mostly of the smaller variety – hare, partridge and pheasant, though venison is occasionally available.

Fine quality poultry also features on the menu. Chicken is the traditional Sunday treat. It is an old custom to serve stuffed goose on St. Martin's Eve, 10th November, followed by *æblekage*, round apple fritters. The Christmas dinner is usually roast duck. Favourite Danish vegetables are red, green and white cabbage – the last is also made into sauerkraut – as well as celeriac, leeks and root vegetables, especially beetroot.

The potato is an important part of the Danish diet. There is even a dish, *nye kartofler*, which consists solely of potatoes. Only small round new potatoes, especially those from the island of Samsø, are used in its preparation. Traditional stews and fried dishes are still popular. Yellow Pea Soup, *gule ærter*, is a great favourite with Danes. It is a meal in itself and is often served to guests. Sometimes ice-cold akvavit and beer are drunk with it.

Herring, *sild*, plays a very important role in Danish cuisine. It is on the table at almost every meal and is prepared in a variety of ways. Buckling is herring smoked over an alder wood fire, giving it a very delicate flavour. Bucking is a speciality of the island of Bornholm.

A typical Dane begins the day early in the morning with a modest first breakfast, called *morgenmad*. This consists of a slice of rye bread or a roll spread with golden salted butter, and topped with a slice of cheese or spread with jam. There may even be time for a Danish pastry.

At around lunchtime, between 12 and 2pm, *frokost*, the "real" breakfast, is eaten. It consists mainly of *smørrebrød*, the Danish open sandwich. A sandwich may sound simple, but in this case it means a thin slice of sour rye or wholewheat bread topped with everything that the heart could desire. The elaborate open sandwiches are a sumptuous meal in themselves.

Nowadays, the main meal of the day is eaten between 6 pm and 8 pm, although in the past the midday meal was the most important one, and this custom still survives in the countryside. That is why this meal is still known as *middag*, i.e. the midday meal. After the day's work is done, the whole family sits down to a hot meal, consisting of soup, a main course and a dessert. The dessert could be a pudding or may be replaced by a savoury piece of cheese. This meal is often rounded off with coffee and Danish pastries, and perhaps a small glass of liqueur, especially when there are guests.

Smørrebrød is a typically Danish invention. The original idea was thought up a long time ago, when peasants and serfs took their lunch with them to the fields. Modern Danes still take their *smørrebrød* to work every day. The open sandwich has to be neatly packed and protected from drying out. Schoolchildren get their *smørrebrød* in a colourful lunchbox which they take with them to school. Homemade *smørrebrød* usually consists of a slice of rye bread spread with butter and topped with cold leftovers, perhaps fish or meat from the previous day's meal, but always attractively garnished with herbs, sliced radish or beetroot.

In the towns, special shops and restaurants display countless varieties of *smørrebrød* assembled into sophisticated, mouth-watering presentations. The sandwich-makers have to undergo a three-year apprenticeship in order to learn how to create these masterpieces.

The Danes demonstrate their true creativity when they prepare *smørrebrød* for parties. There are a few basic rules to observe. The open sandwiches should always look attractive and the colour of the garnishes and the toppings should harmonise with each other. Only ingredients of the finest quality should be used.

The base of the *smørrebrød* is always a thin slice of bread. Rye bread is the most suitable for thick slices of meat, fish and the various cheeses. White bread is used with delicately-flavoured toppings. Mixed wheat-and-rye bread, caraway seed bread, wholewheat bread and crispbread are all put to good use. It is important to have a good crisp crust on the bread. As a rule, the bread slices are spread thickly with salted butter, but if the sandwich contains pork sausages, roast pork, new potatoes or cheese, lard is more appropriate. Seafood toppings for *smørrebrød* include crab, mussels, crayfish or lobster. Roasted or marinated pork, beef or lamb, liver pâté, rissoles, ham or brawn are also very popular. Game and poultry, roasted or in a pâté, always go down well. All kinds of vegetables and salads accompany the main ingredients. Hard-boiled eggs, raw egg yolk, shredded crabmeat, flaked fish and thinly-sliced tomatoes are just some of the toppings.

Denmark has a rich selection of different cheeses. Some of these are particularly suitable for *smørrebrød*. Tybo, Danbo and Elbo are mild, aromatic, medium-hard cheeses. Maribo, on the other hand, is strong-tasting and also slightly sour. Havarti, Esrom and Danish herb cheese are aromatic and spicy.

Samsø and Svenbo are rather full-bodied and nutty. The very mild Danish mozzarella, Akawi and Danish feta are all semi-hard cheeses. Danish Camembert and Brie are white-mould soft cheeses. Danablu and Mycella, the blue-mould and blue-veined cheeses, are full-bodied, highly-flavoured and creamy, like the white-mould soft cheeses. Fresh cheeses can be improved with herbs, seasonings, fruit, nuts, brandy or liqueur. The hard cheeses include Danish Cheddar, Danish Hingino and Grana. These last two are particularly suitable for grating.

When making *Smørrebrød*, slices of meat, fish or cheese should be loosely rolled, before being heaped on the bread, then sprinkled with herbs and seasonings. A lettuce leaf should be used to separate the bread-and-butter from the topping, so that the bread does not soak up any liquid from the ingredients and become soggy. That is why sauces are served separately in small sauceboats. *Smørrebrød* should always be eaten with a knife and fork.

A special children's *Smørrebrød* consists of buttered bread with a sweet topping, such as chocolate with sultanas or puréed banana with chocolate powder. Few adults would turn up their noses at such a treat!

The Danes like to drink beer or ice-cold akvavit with *smørrebrød*. No wonder beer is so popular, with so many small breweries in provincial towns as well as world-famous names like Carlsberg and Tuborg. White wine or red wine can also be drunk with some types of *smørrebrød*, but never with herring. Drivers and anyone who prefers non-alcoholic drinks accompany their sandwiches with low-alcohol beer, mineral water or cold milk. *Velbekomme* – enjoy your meal!

Basic recipe for the yeast puff dough used in Danish pastries:
Mix 60g (2 oz) fresh yeast with 50g (2 oz) sugar and mix with 1/4 litre (8 fl oz) tepid milk. Add 1 whole egg and 1 egg yolk, 1/4 tsp ground cardamom and 1/2 tsp vanilla sugar. Lastly, stir in 500g (1 lb) sifted flour and work into a dough. Wrap the dough in clingfilm and refrigerate it for 1 hour. Roll the dough out into a circle on a floured wooden board and put 250g (8 oz) softened butter, shaped into a flattened rectangle, into the centre of the dough. Now fold the edges of the dough over the butter and roll it out into a rectangle as thick as your finger. Fold the left third of the dough over the middle third and the right third over the other two. Wrap in waxed paper and chill for 15 minutes. Roll the dough out into a rectangle again. This time both sides should be folded into the middle and finally closed like a notebook. Wrap in waxed paper again and chill for 15–20 minutes.
Repeat this process and then chill the pastry again for 1 hour. Now you can go on to make one of the many varieties of Danish pastry.

Norway is a land shaped by ice. The two characteristic types of landscape here are the fjell (fell), the high plains covered in moss, lichen and low bushes, and the fjords, which cut deep into the heart of the country. The 16 km (10 mile) long Geirangerfjord (above) is profoundly impressive.

Yes, We Love This Land

This is a line from the Norwegian National Anthem: *"Ja, vi elsker dette landet"*. If you have never visited Norway, you can have no conception of the beauty of its townscapes and countryside. Its special appeal lies in the sharp contrasts. The coasts are surrounded by a wild sea of which the picturesque fjords are arms extending deep into the mountainous landscape. The steep cliff-faces and the blue-white glaciers are mirrored in the glassy surface of the fjord waters. The valleys, carpeted with flowers in the spring, are dotted here and there with a few isolated farmhouses. They contrast with the craggy, unspoilt landscape of the high plateaux, the fells, and the snow-covered peaks and glaciers which overshadow the valleys.

Telemark, the southernmost part of the country, with its generally mild climate, stretches from the coast to the high mountains and contains features that are typical of Norway. The immense forests are interspersed with well-farmed valleys. The transitions here are not so abrupt as they are further north. The extensive forests provide timber for export. Many of the buildings in the countryside are built of timber, whether they are the mediaeval wooden churches or the centuries-old log-cabin farmhouses, whose timbers are beautifully decorated. Traditional handicrafts and ancient customs, such as silversmithing and "rose painting", have been kept alive to this day.

Finnmark, the northernmost part of Norway, has only a short Scandinavian summer but winter lasts a very long time. Sometimes the night sky is illuminated by the Aurora borealis, with its strange flowing ribbons of light. In this part of the world it is not unusual to experience temperatures well below −40 °C (−40 °F) in mid-winter. Yet when the summer returns, nowhere else are the days so bright or so long as they are here. In Hammerfest, the sun does not set at all between mid-May and the end of July. Nature makes use of this short but intense season by displaying amazing fertility.

Most of Norway is mountainous. The valleys of the Trøndelag district are heavily farmed in contrast with its bare, rugged mountains. The forests contain rivers stocked with fish. There are fjords and off-shore islands. The small fishing villages have featured in the work of the writer Knut Hamsun. Here the summer days last longer than in the southern part of Norway, and in midsummer it doesn't get dark at all. This promotes the rapid growth of wheat, vegetables and fruit. Tomatoes, pears and apples develop a strong flavour. The rugged mountain peaks are famous for being among Norway's richest hunting grounds, and the rivers are reputed by salmon fishermen to be the best in the country.

Although the four million or so inhabitants of Norway live on a large landmass of 324,000 sq. km (125,100 sq. miles), only 3.5 % of the land is suitable for agriculture. A quarter of it is forested and the rest is virtually treeless. The few twisted scrub pines, dwarf birches and juniper bushes peter out at 1,000 m (3,300 ft) in the south, but further north the treeline descends as low as 300 m (1,000 ft). The Norwegians call these treeless regions, *vidda*.

Since the land is rocky and barren, life in Norway has always been hard. This forced the Vikings to look to the surrounding sea for food. It is just the same today. The Norwegians are still ardent seafarers and keen fishermen.

Norway extends from the 58th to the 71st parallel. The distance from north to south is enormous, 1,750 km (1,087 miles), roughly equivalent to the distance from Hamburg to Sicily. The diet thus varies considerably from north to south. Norwegians from the north may be quite unfamiliar with popular southern Norwegian foods. For instance, shellfish are mainly eaten in the south, while northerners love whalemeat steak, a northern delicacy unknown in the south.

Norwegian cuisine is simple and natural, just like the rocky land – and the sea – from which it comes, but it is richly diversified. The food is savoury and delicious, full of unusual and exciting tastes.

Before describing any dishes or recipes in detail, it is a good idea to look at the ingredients that go to make up a typical Norwegian meal, starting with fish.

The dried North Atlantic cod, *tørrfisk* or *stokkfisk* and the salted *klippfisk* has been highly-valued since ancient times, not least for its excellent keeping qualities. Fresh cod, *torsk* in Norwegian, is boiled briefly in plenty of heavily-salted water, and served with boiled potatoes and melted butter. Another favourite fish in Norway is *makrell*, mackerel. It tastes best in the spring, when it is at its plumpest. Mackerel is prepared in several different ways – stuffed with parsley and sautéed, smoked, or even salt-cured as a substitute for the more expensive salmon. Herring is always featured in the Norwegian cold buffet, the *koldbord*. It can be prepared in numerous ways and is easy to serve.

Crab and lobster are extremely popular; they are delicious but expensive. Prawns, available at the fish markets, freshly-landed and ready-cooked, are good value. In restaurants, they are usually served in their shells.

Norway is rich in inland waterways and rivers whose waters are unpolluted. No wonder then that Norwegian cuisine has so many delicious freshwater fish dishes. Salmon, the noblest of fish, whether poached, smoked or salt-cured and served as *gravlax*, is always a special gastronomic experience.

Norwegian lakes and rivers are full of trout which often feature on the menu. One way in which they are prepared is called *rakfisk*. For this, the trout are soaked in brine for several months.

The Norwegians understand better than most how many culinary treats can be devised using fish. One of these delights is *Bergens fiskesuppe*, Bergen Fish Soup. As with classic dishes all over the world, there is no single standard way of making Bergen Fish Soup. Each Norwegian cook has his or her treasured recipe.

Dried fish are often pounded into a creamy white paste and used to make composite fish dishes such as *fiskepudding*, which is usually baked and served with a pink prawn sauce. Other dishes made from pounded, dried fish are *fiskeboller*, fish balls, and *fiskekake*, fishcakes.

This mountainous country with its steep slopes is not ideal for either beef or dairy cattle. It is much more suitable for sheep and goats. Mutton is made into *fenålår*. A leg of mutton is lightly-marinated, then smoked, wrapped in muslin, and dried for several months in an airy attic or hayloft. The meat shrinks to around half its original weight, but the flavour increases proportionately. The mutton is sliced paper-thin and eaten on flat crispbread with fresh, salted butter. The bones can be used in a vegetable stew or to make nourishing stock.

Similar simple dishes remain popular today. The methods of preparation arose from the necessity of using what food there was in the most economical and tasty way possible.

Game dishes are especially popular. The reindeer roam wild in central Norway, whereas in the tundra of the far north they are reared in herds and are semi-domesticated. Wild animals such as elk, red deer, reindeer, hare and game birds, are all hunted in their official open seasons. In each season, the appropriate game is roasted and served with lingonberries or cloudberries. All game dishes are served with a sauce, usually made from fresh and sour cream and melted goat's cheese, *geitost*. Wild mushrooms from the mountain forests are also classic accompaniments.

One of the oldest Norwegian recipes is for porridge, made from almost any cereal available. *Rømmegrøt*, oatmeal porridge, could be considered to be the Norwegian national dish. It is traditionally served at weddings.

These porridges and gruels are the forerunners of bread. There may be many kinds of porridge, but there are even more kinds of bread. This is because small villages and isolated farms were so remote from each other, separated as they were by impassable mountain ranges, that each developed its own recipe and style of bread-making. Most of the breads were round crisp flatbreads, which are still baked in the same way today. They have a robust flavour and are served at every mealtime.

The Norwegian day begins with the first meal, *frokost*, a hearty breakfast. A well-laid out *frokostbord* offers various kinds of bread and countless types of fish. Herring is served in traditional Norwegian style, in a delicious sweet-and-sour sauce made with mustard, pepper, onion rings and bay leaf, with sliced beetroot and perhaps mayonnaise. This is followed by sliced sausages and a variety of salads, fruit and jams. And, of course, there is always *rømmegrøt*. Of the various cheeses, the favourite is *geitost*, the golden-brown goat's cheese. With its mild, distinctive taste, it is a Norwegian speciality.

The midday meal is called the *lunsjbord*. It is even more substantial and varied than the *frokostbord* and includes at least one hot dish, perhaps pork or mutton meatballs, and even a slice of fresh salmon.

The Norwegians eat their main meal in the evening when further delicacies are on offer, such as fresh fish from the coast, roast reindeer meat from the far north, delicious roast elk or snow grouse from inland. A wide variety of vegetables, salads and berry sauces are served with them. *Rømmegrøt* is served again, but this time with melted butter and powdered cinnamon.

To drink, there is beer, low-alcohol beer, mineral water or fresh milk. For those who drink alcohol, the meal can begin and end with a tiny glass of Linie-Akvavit.

Norwegian cooking shows many signs of Danish influence, the result of the long union between the two countries, which only ended in 1814 with the signing of the Treaty of Kiel. When the Hanseatic League was in its heyday, Norwegian cuisine was subjected to much foreign influence, but it has retained many unmistakable original features.

The Norwegian fishing industry is still an important sector of the economy. Herring and cod are the principal fish caught here. There has been a fishing industry in the Lofoten Islands, in the far north, for thousands of years. From January to the end of April, the fishermen put out to sea in their diesel-driven cutters to cast their nets far and wide (opposite: above left and below left). At this time of year, the herring and cod are spawning in the waters around the Lofoten Islands, which are warmed by the Gulf Stream. Once caught, the fish are quickly processed (opposite, and below right). The fish market of the southern Norwegian town of Bergen is justly famous (above). Every working day, the freshly-caught fish are weighed (right), then cut into portions, filleted or sold whole.

Stockholm – the Venice of the North

The Smörgåsbord – Generous Hospitality and Unlimited Variety

Sweden is often associated with the welfare state, equality of women and the free-and-easy behaviour of the younger generation. It is also famous for its high-quality steel. Swedish men and women are all supposed to be blond. However, Sweden is not just a mass of clichés, it is a fascinating country which is a delight to visit. Swedish food is wholesome and delicious. The best introduction to the good food of Sweden is through the *smörgåsbord*, the Swedish cold buffet, proof of the great gastronomic artistry of the Nordic countries.

Amazingly, this magnificent tradition was on the verge of falling into oblivion, but it was helped to new glory and fame by the big hotels and gourmet restaurants. The *smörgåsbord* consists of a sumptuously laden table, which offers all the delicacies you could possibly imagine in one decorative display. The result looks like a colourful still-life of delicious food. It is an impressive example of the variety and lusciousness of Swedish cuisine. *Smörgåsbord* is much more than its simple name implies. Translated, it simply means "bread-and-butter table". At home, when friends are invited or on important occasions such as Christmas, the home-made *smörgåsbord* is the pride of every house wife.

The buffet consists of a succession of dishes which require careful planning, so they are ready to be served in the correct order. As a rule, there are five courses. The starter consists of all the herring combinations imaginable. These are followed by other fish dishes, salads, meats, hot dishes, cheese and desserts.

Herring, *sill*, is traditionally the king of appetisers. It can be served in jelly, or marinated, smoked, grilled, made into Glassblower's Herring, Matjes herring, salt herring, rollmops or buckling. It can also be presented in a mustard marinade. Every method of preparation is a delight to the palate. Garnishes include sliced onion rings, cornichons (miniature gherkins), beetroot, bunches of dill and relishes. Cheese is on the table at this course, and there is a wide selection of wheat and rye breads and crispbreads which can be spread with butter. Small potatoes boiled in their skins are also eaten with herring.

The second course consists of fish, shellfish and crustaceans made into cold hors d'œuvres. Salmon is usually included in many variations, not only salted, as in the famous *gravad lax*, but also smoked, and served with the obligatory fresh mustard sauce. Salmon-trout, eel and caviar may also be served with this course.

The third course consists of numerous, colourful salads. They are placed next to cold cuts, such as boiled or smoked ham, slices of roast game, reindeer, beef, pork and lamb. There may also be boned, stuffed loin of pork, brawn, pâté and sausage. Smoked sausage is popular: it may take the form of the stronglyflavoured, slightly-sour *femmarkerkorv*, or the *herrgårdskorv* "manor-house sausage", or even *spickekorv*, which is similar to salami but saltier and onion-flavoured. A poultry dish may also be served.

The fourth course is the *småvarmt*. This consists of several small, hot dishes, examples of real home cooking, such as Jansson's Temptation – a potato dish flavoured with anchovies and cream – little meatballs or delectable stuffed onion balls.

The last course is based on a selection of fine cheeses, such as *kryddost*, a herb cheese containing caraway and cloves or *sveciaost*, which tastes very mild when young but has a strong, sharp taste when ripe. Alternatively, there is *västerbottenost*, which develops a sharper and sourer taste the older it gets. It is always included in a large buffet. These savouries are followed by fruit salad, fresh fruit, puddings, compotes and the traditional dessert of red berries.

In order to enjoy all this properly, the Swedes abide by the maxim: "eating something good and beautiful gives pleasure when eaten at the right time". You must allow yourself plenty of time. Walk around the table and choose from the various dishes of herring on offer. Resist the temptation to pile your plate high and do take only small portions, so that you will have room to try the largest possible number of dishes and enjoy the *smörgåsbord* to the end. The Swedes enjoy ice-cold akvavit with their herrings. When the herring-plates are removed, they are replaced by another course of fish dishes. The Swedes make a clear distinction between their beloved herring and other fish. The fish course is followed by meat and a selection of salads.

Hot dishes, the *småvarmt* of the *smörgåsbord*, do not feature in the Swedish midday meal. Instead they are served with the main meal of the day, *middag*, synonymous with the evening meal. Milk, cultured milk, mineral water or *öl*, beer, are usually drunk with the meal, and wine is very popular. Like the other countries of Scandinavia, Sweden has strict liquor laws, especially where drinking and driving are concerned.

Next come the cheese and fruit. And after this, for those who can still manage it, there awaits a sweet dessert. But the meal would not be complete without cakes and coffee to finish.

The Swedish *smörgåsbord* invokes the pleasant thought that one has truly entered the land of plenty. It is also an expression of Swedish hospitality. The *smörgåsbord* is so inviting but you need to use some self-control! Although foreign food has recently influenced the Swedish diet, traditional *husmanskost*, or

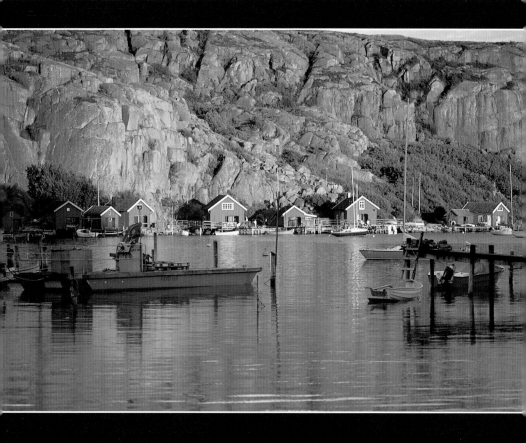

Sweden is a land of unspoilt countryside and magnificent vistas. As it has the largest landmass of all the Scandinavian countries, the landscape varies considerably. There are magnificent inland lakes such as the one shown here (above left).

Öland, off the east coast, is known as the island of windmills. There were once thousands, but now only 400 are left (opposite: below).

With numerous rocky islets and fjords, small bays and beaches, the west coast is one of the most beautiful parts of the country. The little red-painted houses, such as these in Hamburgö (above), are typical of this part of the country.

home cooking, still prevails. The old, well-tried recipes are popular, combined with the fashion for "healthy eating" using fresh, natural foods.

Swedish traditions are at their strongest at Christmas time. The preparations begin in early December, when the smell of Christmas baking and cooking permeates the house to delight the whole family. Christmas Eve is the highlight of the festivities. By early afternoon on 24th December, the festive Christmas *smörgåsbord* is ready and waiting. Then the presents are placed under the Christmas tree. In accordance with ancient tradition, there is dancing in a ring around the tree. After that, the presents are opened and admired. In some families *dopp i grytan*, is served. A slice of rye bread is dipped in hot ham stock, soaked and eaten with ham or small sausages. Afterwards, there is coffee and home-made Christmas cakes. In some homes, the main course at the traditional Christmas evening meal is *lutfisk*. This is cod soaked in wood-ash and dried, then reconstituted and boiled whole. It is eaten with a thick, creamy white sauce.

For dessert there is always rice pudding, *risgrynsgröt*, sprinkled with cinnamon and sugar. The Christmas rice pudding also serves to provide a special kind of entertainment. According to ancient beliefs, it can be used to foretell the future. Housewives mix one sweet and one bitter almond into the pudding, and sometimes add a coin. The person who finds the sweet almond will marry during the coming year. A bitter almond signifies another year as a bachelor. A shiny coin foretells wealth. The Swedes still follow these traditional customs.

The ancient Swedes were hunters, heroes, merchants and farmers. The Svaers, who lived in central Sweden about 2,000 years ago, were hard-working people. They greatly impressed Tacitus, the Roman historian. The Svaers became the dominant tribe in post-Roman times and lent the country its name – *Sverige*.

Sweden has several thousand runestones and burial places of the ancient rulers, known as "ship settlements", all of which are evidence of their rich heritage. Southern Sweden was settled by a German tribe called the Dannæ, later known as the Danes. Their province of Skåne, with its fertile farmland is Sweden's Garden of Eden.

The further north you go in Sweden, the more forested and mountainous the landscape becomes. These forests are home to many types of game. Swedes look forward to the start of the hunting season for elk, deer, hare and wildfowl.

As you near the Arctic Circle, the vegetation becomes sparser and the land more barren. Reindeer moss, lichen and brush predominate. Here the cloudberries ripen during the short summer, along with blackberries, blueberries (bilberries) and cranberries.

Both in respect of landscape and climate, Sweden has been favoured by nature in comparison with neighbouring Norway. The land consists mainly of rolling hills rather than craggy mountain peaks and the rainfall is lower, favouring warmer summers. It was much harder for the missionaries who came here about 1,000 years ago to convince the resident Vikings of the necessity of eating frugally during Lent. The church authorities, so they say, were eventually compelled to grant the grumbling Vikings a solid meal every Tuesday during the Lenten fast. It consisted of roast salt pork with brown beans and a Fasting Tuesday roll, the *fastlagsbulle*, as a dessert. Many Swedes still observe this custom.

The longest day of the year, 24th June, is the occasion for the Midsummer festival, celebrated in the open air with much dancing, good food and drink. The traditional menu consists of *gravad lax*, served with a mustard-and-dill sauce, and roast chicken breast with small, round new potatoes. The main course is accompanied by fresh salad. Strawberries and whipped cream to finish.

There is a soup which deserves a special mention. *Ärtsoppa*, yellow pea-soup may already have been popular in Viking times. According to ancient beliefs, pulses were the favourite food of the Gods. Nowadays in Sweden, yellow pea-soup is served every Thursday in winter. It is followed by jam-filled pancakes for dessert to complete the Swedish national menu. When guests are invited, toasts are drunk in akvavit or cold beer.

– Skål –

A labyrinth of lakes, of afforested islands and inland waterways criss-crosses the Finnish landscape. The "land of a thousand lakes" has a grand total – not including the small ones – of 62,000. In this peaceful and unspoilt landscape the Finns can relax away from the strains of city life.

Of Crayfish and Summer Nights

With five million people and a huge landmass, Finland could hardly be described as densely-populated. The Finnish love of nature makes a lasting impression on the visitor. Finns feel themselves to be part of nature. This is reflected in their cuisine and the ways in which they make use of natural products. Finnish design and style in furnishings, glass, porcelain, ceramics and textiles is elegantly simple but captivatingly beautiful and justly world-renowned. Finnish style is unique, even in Scandinavia.

Finnish handicrafts achieved international recognition and fame at the Paris Exposition Universelle in 1900, when they were widely seen abroad for the first time. This was hardly surprising, since the Finns had been accustomed for centuries to make all their utensils themselves. Their isolation in villages surrounded by huge forests compelled them to do so. Children learnt how to use the Finnish knife to make carvings from an early age. Their skills as craftsmen and their creativity were thus developed from childhood and brought to a high degree of perfection. After the Milan Exhibition of 1957, exports of Finnish handicrafts enjoyed another boom.

This industrious and talented people migrated from central Asia more than 2,000 years ago, and settled in the area around the Baltic, gradually advancing further and further northwards. They traded with their neighbours in valuable animal furs. The original inhabitants, the *Same,* were pushed even further north.

The importance of fur trading in Finland has declined, but many Finns continue to live off the land. Today, more than a quarter of them still earn a livelihood from farming and forestry. In the summers, the farmers work their land. Winter is the time for cutting timber in the forests, when the snow makes it easy to transport the logs. In the spring, when the lakes and rivers are free of ice, the trunks are lashed together to make enormous rafts which are floated down to the coast. It pays to export. With almost 20 million hectares (50 million acres) of forest, Finland is the third-largest timber-exporting nation in Europe, after Sweden and the former Soviet Union. In the south the timber consists mainly of spruce and deciduous trees, but as you travel northwards pine and birch trees predominate, interspersed with scrub. It is here that the berry bushes flourish best.

Blueberries (bilberries), cranberries, lingonberries and cloudberries (known as *lakkoja*) play an important part in the Finnish diet, next only to mushrooms. The Finns love the wild, tart natural taste of these berries, so it is not surprising that many meals end with a berry pudding. Lingonberries are plentiful in the forests. They are similar to cranberries in taste and appearance, but are smaller and have a somewhat resinous flavour. They are served with meat dishes, particularly roast game. The somewhat larger cranberries, which grow throughout the country, are also popular with meat, because of their tart flavour. In the autumn the air is filled with the heady perfume of ripening berries. However, cranberries are generally picked early in the year, after the spring thaw.

North of the treeline, the vegetation slowly changes into tundra. Here even the birches find it hard to stand their ground and at this point become stunted and bush-like. They are replaced by moss and lichen on which the reindeer feed. The semi-domesticated reindeer, reared in large herds, together with fish, form the basis of the *Same* diet.

In southern and central Finland, extensive moorland and swamps are interspersed with forests and lakes. With a little luck, you may encounter an elk, the largest wild animal in the country, or might glimpse a wolf or a bear. Naturally, fish abound in the land of a thousand lakes. Salmon and trout enrich the

There are many stories and legends about the elk, the most stately and majestic animal in the Nordic regions. One of these tells how the elk originally came down to Earth from Heaven as a six-legged animal but moved so fast that no mortal could catch it. In fact, despite its enormous weight, the elk can reach incredible speeds effortlessly. Its projecting palmated antlers can reach a span of up to 2 metres (6 ft).

menu, and baked pike is a great delicacy. The deep-sea fishing industry relies mainly on cod and Baltic herring.

The Finns love to commune with nature, especially in high summer. This is the time of the crayfish harvest from the countless rivers and lakes. The annual traditional crayfish feast finds the Finns on the wooded shores enjoying this festival in merry groups.

A stroll through a market in a small Finnish town is both fascinating and instructive, giving a good insight into the kind of food the country has to offer. Various kinds of vegetables are displayed on the stalls to their best advantage, and all look fresh and inviting. There are bright-red tomatoes, mountains of yellow swedes and bunches of white radishes, heads of white and red cabbage, green cucumbers and bunches of celery, all fresh and carefully cleaned. Bunches of herbs, especially dill, are on offer in a peasant woman's basket. Finns love flowers and plants so a market will always have lots of flower stalls. The berries – blueberries (bilberries), cloudberries, lingonberries and cranberries – are displayed in trays. The cloudberries, which tend to turn to liquid, are kept fresh in special, watertight wooden tubs. More tubs are filled with salted mushrooms or pickles. Another stall is piled with fresh fruit, apples, pears and plums, all beautifully polished and appetisingly displayed. Wildfowl are hanging here, salted and fresh fish are on offer over there.

The market is an important meeting place for Finns, but it is not noisy. Finns seem to be able to say a great deal without doing much talking. Whether big or small, old or young, they like to sit watching the world go by, as if constantly waiting for something. Perhaps they have a calm philosophy of life, an attitude which has been lost elsewhere in the bustle of the modern world. Their calm, stoical approach to life, which they refer to as *sisu*, translates most appropriately as "the ability to stay the course". The Finns are very hard-working and persevering and need all the determination they can muster to cope with their harsh climate.

One favourite dish is porridge. The Finnish version is thick, robust and well-flavoured. One of the most delicious varieties consists of pot barley stewed for several hours in milk until it is soft and has developed a reddish-brown colour. It is eaten with berries or a rose-hip purée. There are many other kinds of gruels and porridges, some of them made from a mixture of grains. *Talkkuna*, for example, consists of grain simmered in salted-water, then dried in the heat from the sauna stove or in a cooling bread-oven. This makes it easy to grind into flour for gruel *(velli)*.

Finland also has a rich variety of breads, which vary from district to district, in terms of type and flavour. In the western part of the country, perhaps partly due to Swedish influence, the bread is flat, hard and crisp. The hole in the middle served in former times to thread the bread on to poles, so that it could be stored in the attic or granary. In the eastern part of the country, the bread is more typically a sour-dough rye, of a type also found in Russia and central Europe.

Finnish cuisine has been moulded by influences from East and West. In the 12th century, Finland was conquered by Sweden. It eventually became a province of Sweden with equal rights, Turku being the provincial capital. This brought Finland into the mainstream of mediaeval European culture. Finland remained linked to Sweden for the next 600 years, which naturally had a lasting influence on the country's eating traditions. In this context, it is interesting to note that the Finnish equivalent of the Swedish *smörgåsbord* is called *voileipäpöytä*.

Much of the Russian influence on Finnish cuisine was introduced after 1809, when Sweden was forced to surrender its Finnish province to Russia. Karelia, part of eastern Finland, became the connecting link to the gastronomic culture of the East. Countless recipes, some of them very good, entered into Finnish cuisine. One example is the traditional Easter pudding, *mämmi*, which is prepared from rye flour, rye salt, sugar beet syrup, bitter orange peel, salt and water. The preparation requires patience and skill. It tastes best after it has been allowed to mature for several days. The dish is eaten cold, sprinkled with sugar and served with single cream. In former times, this Easter dish was served in containers made of birch bark (tuohi). *Pasha* is a Russian desert made from cream cheese and served at Easter; the name, in fact, means "Easter".

Another speciality of Karelian cuisine is the *piirakka*, a kind of pie or pasty, which can take various forms. The name is derived from the Russian word, *pirog*. A Karelian *piirakka* is a flat round of rye dough, topped with thick rice porridge or mashed potato. The edges are folded towards the centre and crimped, leaving the filling partially exposed. They are frequently brushed with melted butter during baking and are served hot, either with more melted butter or with a delicious sauce of mashed hard-boiled eggs and melted butter.

A special kind of pie is baked in the province of Savo in central Finland. It is called *kalakukko* and looks like a large round rye loaf, but contains a rich and delicious filling. The filling consists of several small fish called *muikku*, a relative of the salmon which only lives in fresh water, though other freshwater fish can be used. The fish are cleaned but not boned. After seasoning them with salt, strips of fatty pork are laid on top of them and the dough sealed around them. They are then baked in a slow oven until the bones of the fish dissolve. A similar dish, cooked in a casserole sealed with a lid of rye dough, is called *patakukko*.

Gratins and stews are very popular in Finland. *Lanttulaatikko* is a swede gratin, swede being a favourite vegetable in Finland. It is an old custom to include this dish in the Christmas menu. The abundance of fish in the many Finnish waters, and the native passion for fishing, contribute to another nourishing dish, *kalapata*, a fish stew. Such dishes also had their practical side. Once the bread had been baked in a very hot oven, the heat could still be used for cooking, while the cook went off to work in the field or forest.

Other Russian specialities which feature in the Finnish diet include the famous cabbage borscht soup and meat kebabs, briefly grilled over an open fire.

Finland's favourite drinks are beer and milk. It is by no means rare for the beer to be home-brewed. Akvavit is less popular than in the rest of Scandinavia, its place being taken by Finnish vodka.

If you enjoy pure, natural food prepared from the finest ingredients, then you will love Finnish cuisine. Finns still eat what their ancestors enjoyed hundreds of years ago, food which kept them healthy and offered them longevity.

A quarter of a million people live in Lapland. Almost as many reindeer as
human beings wander through it, across the national borders of the countries it
covers. There is an old saying, "Reindeer, Lapland and the Same go together
like tobacco, fire and a pipe", indispensable features of every Same's life.
Above: Reindeer and a Pulkka sled, once the traditional means of transport
during the winter in Lapland. However, technology is forging ahead even here.
Motorized sleighs are replacing the reindeer-pulled variety.

Eel in Beer Sauce

Ål med ölsås
Sweden

The Swedes love food from the sea, lakes and rivers. One of the favourite Swedish delicacies is eel.

The eels' spawning ground lies in the middle of the Atlantic, in the area commonly known as the Sargasso Sea. After the eels have spawned there the older generation dies. The developing larvae begin a journey that will last many years, until the elvers finally reach Europe and the Swedish coastal and inland waters. At this point they are about 6 centimetres (2 inches) long. It will be seven to 10 years before they are fully grown. The fully-grown adults will travel back to spawn in the Sargasso Sea, where the lifecycle will begin again. At the autumn Eel Festival, these delicacies are served in a variety of ways – boiled, grilled, fried, roasted and smoked. And of course, they must always be accompanied by a glass of akvavit.

*1 kg (2 lb) eels, 375 ml (12 fl oz) beer,
1 onion, 4 peppercorns, 1 bay leaf,
1 piece untreated lemon peel, 1 sprig dill,
salt, 30 g (1 oz) butter, 25 g (3/4 oz) flour,
pepper*

Clean, gut, wash and skin the eels and cut them into pieces about 6 cm (2 inches) long. Bring the beer containing the finely chopped onion and flavourings to the boil. Salt the eel pieces, put them into the liquid, cover and let them poach on very low heat for 20 minutes. Melt the butter in another pan, add the flour and make a roux. Strain the stock, stir it into the roux and cook for a few minutes. Season with salt and pepper. Finally, add the eel pieces to the sauce and serve hot.

Swedish Applecake

Svensk äppelkaka
Sweden

The Swedes are very fond of sweet cakes and pastries. They are eaten as snacks with a cup of coffee or to round off the meal. Second helpings are seldom refused!
Svensk äppelkaka is not really a cake at all, but a dessert. It is either served hot, straight from the oven, with a vanilla sauce similar to custard or with lightly-whipped fresh cream, to which a little sour cream is added. Both are delicious accompaniments.

60g (2 oz) sultanas, 3 tbsp rum,
120g (4 oz) butter, 60g (2 oz) sugar,
1 sachet (10–15g) vanilla sugar, 2 eggs,
100g (3 1/2 oz) ground almonds,
grated rind and juice of 1/2 untreated
lemon, 1/2 tsp cinnamon,
5–6 apples (depending on size),
butter for greasing the dish

Soak the sultanas in the rum. Cream the butter, sugar and vanilla sugar. Separate the eggs. Add the yolks, ground almonds, grated lemon rind and cinnamon to the creamed butter. Beat the egg whites until stiff and fold into the mixture. Peel and core the apples, cut them into slices and sprinkle them with the lemon juice. Butter a fireproof dish, arrange the apples in a fan shape and cover with the rum-soaked sultanas. Spread the almond mixture over the top and bake in a preheated oven at 180–200°C (350–400°F, gas mark 4–6) for about 20 minutes.

THE BLUE DOOR

Sale

11 – 19 February

Friday to Saturday 10 – 5 p.m.

74 CHURCH ROAD BARNES LONDON SW13 0DQ
TEL: 020-8748 9785   FAX: 020-8563 1043

Apple Soup

Æblesuppe
Denmark

When golden autumn arrives and the trees are laden with fruit, some Danish housewives enhance the evening meal with a special kind of soup. Fruit soups are valued above all for their refreshing flavour. Apple soup is a favourite.
This Danish apple soup tastes just as good hot or cold.

600 g (1 1/4 lb) apples, 1 vanilla pod,
500 ml (16 fl oz) cider,
1 1/2–2 tbsp cornflour mixed with 4 tbsp cold
water, pinch of cinnamon,
sugar to taste according to the sweetness of
the apples, grated rind and juice of
1/2 untreated lemon, 1–2 tbsp akvavit,
125 ml (4 fl oz) whipped fresh cream

Peel, core and quarter the apples and put them into 500 ml (16 fl oz) water. Split the vanilla pod and scrape it out over the pot, then add it to the apples. When the apples are soft, after about 15 minutes, discard the vanilla pod. Purée the apple with the liquid or pass them through a sieve. Add the cider. Thicken with the cornflour mixture and briefly bring to the boil. Flavour with cinnamon, sugar, lemon juice and lemon rind and round off with the akvavit. Serve garnished with dollops of whipped cream.

Beer Soup

Øllebrød
Denmark

Beer soup is a Danish speciality, and is served at breakfast as well as on special occasions. If you should ever receive an invitation to eat with a Danish family, you will love the flavour of this soup.
Beer soups are also popular in the other Scandinavian countries, though the ingredients and methods of preparation may vary.

5 tbsp grated stale black bread,
750 ml (1 1/4 pints) malt beer,
1 1/2 tbsp sugar, 1/2 tsp vanilla sugar,
1 piece cinnamon stick, pinch of salt,
1/4 untreated lemon, 2 egg yolks,
250 ml (8 fl oz) fresh cream

Add the beer, sugar, vanilla sugar, cinnamon stick, salt and lemon to the bread and let them cook over a low heat, stirring occasionally. Remove the cinnamon stick and lemon. Beat the egg yolks with half the cream and a ladleful of the liquid. Remove the hot soup from the heat and stir this mixture into it. Stir until thickened.
Whip the cream and top each portion of soup with a dollop of cream.

Bornholm Salad

Salat Bornholm
Denmark

Is it any wonder that herring, the type of fish most frequently caught off the Scandinavian coast, is also the one prepared in the greatest variety of ways?
If you feel like eating something filling which doesn't require too much preparation, then Bornholm salad is just the thing. Beer is often drunk with it.

3 smoked herrings (buckling).
For the sauce:
1 small onion, 1/2 bunch parsley, 1 bunch dill, 1 bunch chives, 2 tbsp vinegar, 1/2 tsp salt, pinch of freshly ground white pepper, 4 tbsp oil, 1/2 tbsp tomato ketchup, 1 tbsp sour cream, 2 tbsp fresh cream. 3 hard-boiled eggs, 1 tomato

Bone the buckling.
To make the sauce: finely chop the onion and most of the herbs, reserving a few sprigs of parsley and dill for the garnish. Stir the salt and pepper into the vinegar. Gradually stir in the oil, tomato ketchup and the fresh and sour cream. Add the diced onion and chopped herbs.
Layer the herring fillets and the slices of hard-boiled egg in a dish, coat the mixture with the sauce and leave to marinate in the refrigerator for at least two hours.
Garnish with herbs and tomato segments.

Cold Buttermilk Soup

Kærnemælkskoldskål
Denmark

Milk products are very popular in Scandinavia. The preparation of sour milk products reflects a particularly ancient tradition. Even today, much more milk is drunk in the Nordic countries than elsewhere in Europe. A visit to a Danish *mælkbar*, one of the numerous milk bars, provides a wide variety of appetizing products to savour.

*60 g (2 oz) sultanas, 3 tbsp sherry,
2 egg yolks, 50 g (2 oz) sugar,
1 tbsp lemon juice,
grated rind of 1/2 untreated lemon,
60 g (2 oz) ground almonds,
1 litre (1 3/4 pints) buttermilk,
125 ml (4 fl oz) whipped fresh cream*

Soak the sultanas in the sherry. Whisk the egg yolks and sugar. Add the lemon juice, lemon rind, ground almonds and buttermilk, stirring constantly. Finally, add the sultanas, and serve the soup well chilled, decorated with dollops of cream.

Roast Haunch of Elk with Chanterelles

Elgstek
Norway

In Norway and Sweden, the term "game" is often used to mean elk meat. With a little luck, you may encounter these magnificent creatures, which mainly live in the northern regions, in their wild habitat.
Venison can be substituted for elk.

1 kg (2–2 1/2 lb) elk haunch.
For the marinade:
500 ml (16 fl oz) red wine, 3 tbsp oil,
5 juniper berries, 2 crushed allspice berries,
1 bay leaf, salt.
4 tbsp oil, 1 onion, 1 carrot,
1 piece of celeriac,
200 g (7 oz) streaky bacon rashers (rinds removed), 500 g (1 lb) chanterelle mushrooms (cleaned and sliced),
125 ml (4 fl oz) fresh cream,
a few drops Worcester Sauce

Prepare the marinade and let the meat soak in it overnight. Allow to drain, reserving the marinade, pat dry and brown in the hot oil. Add the finely-chopped onion, carrot and celeriac and then arrange the bacon rashers over the roast. Pour a little of the marinade over the meat and roast in the oven at 190 °C (375 °F, gas mark 5) for 2 hours or more, basting about every 15 minutes with more marinade. Twenty minutes before the end of the cooking time, add the chanterelle mushrooms.
Blend the cream with the cooking juices in the pan, flavour with Worcester Sauce and serve as a sauce.

Hearty Pea Soup

Ärter och fläsk
Sweden

Dried green and yellow peas can be found all over the world. But it seems that hundreds of years ago, the Swedes opted for dried yellow peas.
The custom of eating pea soup on Thursdays in winter goes back to an old Viking belief. They thought that this pulse was a favourite food of the gods. So to appease the god Thor, dried peas were cooked on Thursdays. This dish is often served to honour a special guest, especially as it goes well with akvavit and beer.

300g (10 oz) yellow splitpeas,
2 litres (3 1/2 pints) water, salt,
white pepper, marjoram, thyme,
1 onion, (finely-chopped), 1 ham bone,
600g (1 1/4 lb) shoulder of pork,
1 leek, 2 carrots,
150g (5 oz) celeriac (thinly sliced),
1 bunch parsley (chopped)

Wash the peas and leave them to soak overnight in the water. The following day, bring the water and peas to the boil, together with the herbs and seasonings, the finely chopped onion and the ham bone. After simmering for a good hour, add the shoulder of pork and the vegetables, and continue to simmer for a further 1 1/2 hours. Remove the ham bone. Remove the pork and cut it into cubes, then return the cubes to the soup. Check the seasoning and add the chopped parsley.
Finns like to add mustard to this soup.

Dried Ling Casserole

Lutfisk
Sweden

Lutfisk is ling or young codfish soaked in woodash and dried in the sun and wind. It owes its somewhat unusual flavour to this ageold method of preserving. Although it is no longer necessary to store fish in this way for the long cold winters, this fish dish remains part of the traditional fare in Scandinavia, particularly Sweden and Finland.
As with rice pudding, many families also eat lutfisk at Christmas. This old custom goes back to the days before the Reformation, when it was usual to fast during Advent.

1 kg (2–2 1/2 lb) lutfisk, 1 sprig thyme,
2 bay leaves, 8 potatoes, 3 onions,
40 g (1 1/2 oz) butter, several sprigs dill,
500 ml (16 fl oz) fresh cream,
white pepper

Leave the fish to soak for at least 5 to 6 hours, changing the water several times. Then put the fish on the stove in a pan of fresh, cold water. Add the thyme and bay leaves, bring slowly to the boil and leave to cook for 12 to 15 minutes. Remove the skin and any bones and slice the fish into 5–6 cm (2–2 1/2 inch) pieces. Cook the potatoes in their skins, peel and cut into slices. Fry the chopped onions in three-quarters of the butter. Use the rest of the butter to grease a fireproof dish. Fill the dish with layers of potato slices, fish pieces and onion, and sprinkle with the chopped dill. Season the cream with a little pepper and pour this over the fish. Bake for about 45 minutes at 160–170 °C (310–325 °F, gas mark 2 1/2–3). Serve with mustard and fresh green peas.

Fish Pie

Kalakukko
Finland

Kalakukko originated in central Finland. It is claimed that the country's best fish pie is obtainable in the marketplace of Kuopio. The rye flour pastry keeps it fresh for a long time. Here, cod has been substituted for *muikku* or *alisen*, which are hard to find outside Finland, if they are available their use is recommended.

For the pastry:
300 g (10 oz) wheat flour, 450 g (1 lb) rye flour, 150 g (5 oz) softened butter, salt, about 375 ml (12 fl oz) water.
For the filling:
750 g–1 kg (1 1/2–2 lb) cod, juice of 1/2 lemon, salt, 250 g (8 oz) boned pork, 150 g (5 oz) bacon, 1/2 bunch dill, 1/2 bunch parsley, pepper
150 g (5 oz) melted butter

To make the pastry: sift the flour and work it into a fairly stiff dough with the butter, salt and water. Leave it to rest for one hour.

To make the filling: gut, clean and bone the cod. Cut the fish into 5-cm (2-inch) pieces, sprinkle it with lemon juice and season with salt. Cut the pork into cubes and sprinkle them with salt. Place the dough onto a floured board and roll it out into a sheet. Brush with melted butter. Arrange the fish and meat in the centre of the dough. Top it with the cubed bacon and chopped herbs, and season with salt and pepper. Brush the edges of the dough with water, fold it over the filling, press well together, and prick with a knitting needle. Brush with melted butter and bake in a pre-heated oven at 200 °C (400 °F, gas mark 6) for 2 hours. During baking, the pastry should be brushed several times with melted butter. After baking the pie for 2 hours, cover it loosely with aluminium foil and reduce the temperature to 170 °C (320 °F, gas mark 3).

Fish Pudding

Fiskepudding
Norway

Norwegian cuisine has much to offer in the way of fish recipes, with its variety of salted and smoked fish, fish salads and fish puddings. These last are evidence of the creativity of the Norwegians, who have conjured up numerous and richly diverse dishes from the harvest of the sea.

1 kg (2–2 1/2 lb) white fish fillets (Baltic or North Atlantic cod, hake, haddock), 125 ml (4 fl oz), fresh cream, 1 egg, 50 g (2 oz) melted butter, 3 tbsp potato flour (farina), 3 tbsp chopped dill, salt, pepper, few drops of Worcester Sauce, butter for greasing pudding basin, 2 tbsp breadcrumbs, several sprigs dill

Blend the cleaned, filleted fish with the cream and egg in a food processor. Add the melted butter, potato flour and dill. Season with salt, pepper and Worcester Sauce.
Butter a pudding basin, sprinkle it with breadcrumbs and fill with the fish mixture. Alternatively, one can substitute a fireproof dish, which would then have to be covered with aluminium foil. Put the pudding basin into a water-bath in the oven, and steam for 1 to 1 1/2 hours. The water should only simmer, and must on no account boil. Test with a skewer or knitting needle. When the skewer comes out clean, the pudding is ready. Before turning out, leave to rest for a few minutes. Garnish with dill sprigs.
Shrimp sauce goes well with this dish.

Bergen Fish Soup

Bergens fiskesuppe
Norway

The special attraction of most Norwegian towns is that they are located on the wild rugged coast, where the fishing boats land their fresh catch daily. Often the housewife is able to buy fish direct from the boat for the midday meal. Bergen fish soup was created in the old port of Bergen, and the recipe has been passed on by word of mouth from generation to generation.

2 onions, 200g (7 oz) carrots, 1 potato,
1 piece celeriac , 1 leek, 1 stick celery,
1 litre (1 3/4 pints) fish stock (made from the
heads and bones of turbot and/or salmon),
600g (1 1/4 lb) fish (cod, haddock, halibut,
salmon, preferably at least two different fish),
juice of 1/2 lemon, salt, 3 egg yolks,
125 ml (4 fl oz) fresh cream,
125 ml (4 fl oz) sour cream,
white pepper, parsley

Chop the onions, slice the carrots, potato and celeriac into small cubes, slice the leek and celery, and cook them in the fish stock for about 12 minutes. Sprinkle the cleaned, washed and boned fish with lemon juice and season with salt. Cut it into pieces and add to the vegetables in the stock. Poach for about 12 minutes over a low heat. Whisk the egg yolks with the cream, sour cream and half a cup (about 125 ml or 4 fl oz) of the fish stock. Remove the stock from the heat and add the mixture to the soup, whisking well until it thickens. Season with salt and pepper and serve sprinkled with chopped parsley.

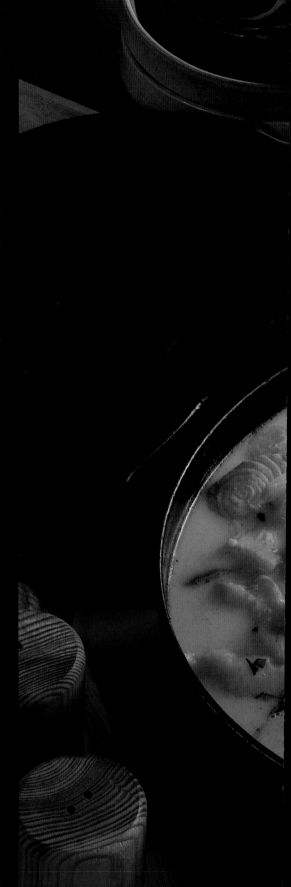

Fish Stew

Kalapata
Finland

The short but intense Finnish summer yields a rich harvest. This is the season when people are able to enjoy the wild foods they find in the countryside. In the land of a thousand lakes this includes fish, of course, but it also includes grains and cereals, such as rye.
Today, home-caught fish and home-baked rye bread are still a tradition in Finland, giving this simple, nourishing fish stew a special touch.

1.25 kg (2 3/4 lb) fish (freshwater fish or small Baltic herrings),
juice of 1/2 lemon, salt, 1 onion, 1 leek,
1 carrot, 1 small piece celeriac,
a few sprigs parsley, dill and chives,
6 allspice berries, 1 bay leaf,
50 g (2 oz) butter, 500 ml (16 fl oz) water

Gut the fish and wash them. If the fish are small leave them whole, but otherwise slice the fish into pieces. Sprinkle it with lemon juice and season with salt. Chop the vegetables and herbs. Bring the water to the boil and add the fish, vegetables, herbs, seasoning and butter. Cook the stew in the oven preheated to 150–160 °C (300–310 °F, gas mark 2–2 1/2) for about 1 hour.
To serve, pass round home-baked rye bread, which is dunked in the fish broth. As a variation, use half the amount of water and substitute single cream.

Small Meatballs

Små köttbullar
Sweden

Although fish predominates in Scandinavian menus, many meat dishes are also noteworthy. A Swedish smörgåsbord is hardly complete without these little spicy meatballs. Served hot with accompanying vegetables, they become a main course. Using good, lean mince, the housewife can prepare a quick and ever-welcome meal.

1 onion, 20g (3/4 oz) butter,
5 tbsp breadcrumbs,
4–5 tbsp fresh cream, 3 tbsp water,
1 egg, 450g (1 lb) minced meat (half beef,
half pork), 1 tbsp chopped chives, salt,
ground cloves, white pepper,
butter for frying.
For the sauce:
30g (1 oz) flour, 250ml (8 fl oz) meat stock,
250ml (8 fl oz) fresh cream

Sauté the finely chopped onion in the butter until soft and translucent. Soak the breadcrumbs in the water and cream. Add the onion, soaked breadcrumbs and the egg to the minced meat, mix well together and season. With wet hands, form little balls and fry in the butter in a pan, browning well on all sides. Remove and keep warm.

To make the sauce: stir the flour into the fat in the frying pan and brown it a little. Stir in the meat stock. Add the cream and let the sauce cook, covered, for about 10 minutes.

The meatballs can be served hot with the cream sauce, or cold as a starter or as cocktail balls. If they are formed into walnut-size balls, they can be eaten with pickled cucumbers and tomatoes in a Swedish smörgåsbord.

Karelian Meat Stew

Karjalan paisti
Finland

The Karelian summer can be quite hot, despite the northern latitude. The sun does not really set from early June to early August. In this short time, nature unfolds in all its splendour. Flowers bloom and the crops, wild berries and fruits ripen.

One of the best-known dishes produced by this area famous for its hospitality is *Karjalan paisti*, a rich meat stew equally suitable for family meals and festive occasions.

200 g (7 oz) lamb, 200 g (7 oz) veal,
200 g (7 oz) beef, 200 g (7 oz) pork,
2 onions, 1 stick celery,
500 g (1 lb) carrots,
600 g (1 1/4 lb) potatoes, 500 g (1 lb) mixed
wild mushrooms (or substitute cultivated
mushrooms),
6 tbsp oil, 1 bay leaf, 4 allspice berries,
about 1.5 litres (2 1/2 pints) stock, salt

Cut the meat into large cubes, the onion into rings, the celery into small cubes and the carrots, potatoes and mushrooms into slices. Fry the meat briefly in the hot oil. Add the onions, celery, bay leaf and allspice. Stir in half the stock, season with salt, and cover the pot. Braise for 1 1/2 hours in a preheated oven at 160–170 °C (310–325 °F, gas mark 2 1/2–3). Then add the carrots, potatoes, mushrooms and the rest of the stock, and leave in the oven for another 40 minutes.

In Karelia, the meat is stewed in a cast-iron pot, but other kinds of ovenproof casseroles with tight-fitting lids are equally suitable.

Trout in Foil Packets

Forell i folie
Sweden

Have you ever watched a Swedish fisher-
man prepare and cook the trout he has just
caught?
He makes a blazing wood fire, and when the
flames have died down, he places the trout,
wrapped in wet newspaper and garnished
with herbs, into the embers. If you are lucky,
he will invite you to share his meal which you
will find really memorable.

4 trout, 1 lemon, salt,
50 g (2 oz) softened butter,
2 bunches dill, pepper

Gut the fish and wash them, then sprinkle
them with lemon juice and season with salt.
Lightly butter four sheets of aluminium foil,
large enough to loosely wrap the fish. Chop
the dill and mix it with the rest of the butter.
Season with salt and pepper. Place each trout
on a prepared sheet of foil and dot each with a
quarter of the dill butter. Carefully wrap each
foil packet, folding to ensure the melted butter does not run out and bake in a medium
oven or wood stove for about 20–25 minutes.
Open the packets and serve in the foil.

Danish Rissoles

Frikadeller
Denmark

Rissoles are quite an important item on the weekly menu and every Danish housewife has a wide repertoire of secret recipes for them. Since the Danes are a very practical and economical people, any leftover rissoles become the basis for the next day's *smørrebrød* or open sandwiches.

1 onion, 250g (1/2 lb) minced pork,
250g (1/2 lb) minced beef,
50g (1 oz) breadcrumbs,
20g (3/4 oz) wheat flour,
1 egg, 60ml (2 fl oz) fresh cream,
60ml (2 fl oz) soda water,
3 tbsp chopped parsley, salt,
freshly ground white pepper,
a little nutmeg (optional),
3 tbsp oil, 30g (1 oz) butter

Dice the onion and mix it with the meat, breadcrumbs, flour, egg, cream, soda water and parsley. Season with salt, pepper and nutmeg, cover loosely with a damp cloth and leave to rest for half an hour. Heat the oil, add the butter and form the mixture into patties. Fry the rissoles for about 7–8 minutes on each side. In Denmark, frikadeller are eaten with potato salad or boiled potatoes and pickled beetroot.

For smørrebrød: The rissoles are eaten arranged on wholemeal rye bread with red cabbage and pickled gherkins.

Roast Goose

Stekt gås
Sweden

On St. Martin's Eve, 10th November, an enticing aroma wafts out from most Swedish homes. It is an old custom to roast a goose stuffed with apples and prunes.

For 6–7 persons:
1 goose (about 5 kg; 11 lb), salt,
freshly ground black pepper,
700 g (1 1/2 lb) apples,
200 g (7 oz) prunes (stoned and soaked in
black tea overnight),
50 g (2 oz) sultanas, 4 tbsp breadcrumbs,
mugwort, 250 ml (8 fl oz) water,
250 ml (8 fl oz) stock, 1 wineglass red wine,
60 ml (4 fl oz) fresh cream,
2 tsp cornflour (optional), marjoram

Wash the drawn and plucked goose and pat it dry with kitchen paper. Rub the bird inside and out with salt and pepper. Chop the heart, liver and gizzard of the goose into small pieces. Slice the apples and prunes and mix them with the sultanas and breadcrumbs. Flavour with a little mugwort. Stuff the goose with this mixture and skewer or sew up the opening. Place the bird on the rack of a roasting pan. Pour water into the bottom of the pan and cook the goose for not more than 3 hours in a preheated oven at 170 °C (325 °F, gas mark 3), checking occasionally to ensure that the water has not evaporated. In the last 20 minutes, sprinkle the goose with cold water and raise the temperature to 220 °C (425 °F, gas mark 7). This will make the skin especially crisp. Remove the fat from the roasting juices, add the stock, red wine and cream and boil to reduce the liquid. Then blend in the cornflour. Season with salt, pepper and a little marjoram.
Chestnut stuffing or a mixture of chestnut and apple stuffing are also suitable.

The Professor's Grog

Professorns glögg
Sweden

This toddy is definitely a winter warmer, just right for the time of year when life goes on mostly behind windowpanes decorated with patterns of frost while blizzards rage outside. The *glögg* should be prepared from an old recipe. It is very conducive to a convivial atmosphere, and is particularly appropriate for Christmas.

For 10 people:
750 ml (1 1/4 pints) red wine,
750 ml (1 1/4 pints) muscatel wine,
250 ml (8 fl oz) white vermouth,
1/2 tbsp angostura bitters,
80 g (1 1/2 oz) sultanas,
grated rind and juice of 1 untreated orange,
1/2 tsp cardamom seeds, 4 cloves,
1 stick cinnamon, 1 piece ginger,
60 g (1 oz) blanched and peeled almonds,
120 g (4 oz) sugar, 1 liqueur glass akvavit

Mix all the ingredients except the sugar and akvavit, and leave to infuse for 10–12 hours. Then add the remaining ingredients. Heat the *glögg* and serve hot in glasses.

Redcurrants and Raspberries with Cream

Rødgrød med fløde
Denmark

A favourite Scandinavian dessert is this simple berry dish served with cream. The Danes use these appetizing red berries in a variety of different ways.

400g (14 oz) redcurrants,
500g (1 lb) raspberries,
up to 750ml (1 1/4 pints) blackcurrant juice,
100g (3 1/2 oz) sugar (according to taste and
the sweetness of the fruit),
70–80g (2 1/2–2 3/4 oz) cornflour,
250ml (8 fl oz) fresh cream, vanilla sugar

Bring the redcurrants and raspberries to the boil with the sugar and all but 3 tablespoons of the blackcurrant juice. Mix the reserved juice with the cornflour. Boil the fruit for 3 minutes, then pour the fruit and cooking juices through a sieve. Stir the cornflour mixture into the resulting purée and return it to the heat. Bring to the boil again.
Serve with lightly whipped cream flavoured with vanilla sugar. If you prefer whole raspberries and redcurrants, you can add a few more whole fresh ones at the end.

Cucumber Salad

Gurksalat
Norway

The Norwegians have always had a special relationship with the gifts of nature. They respect them and handle them with care.
The cucumber is a favourite vegetable in the Norwegian kitchen.
Cucumber salad should always be freshly-made and not left standing around for too long. Do not sprinkle the cucumber slices with salt or they will lose too much liquid.

1 cucumber.
__For the dressing:__
2 tbsp vinegar, salt, pepper,
pinch of sugar, 5 tbsp oil.
2 tbsp fresh dill, 1 tbsp borage

Peel the cucumber from the thick to the thin end. Cut off any bitter part, which can sometimes be found at the thin end in cucumbers not grown under glass. If the cucumbers are small, new and unsprayed, the skin can also be eaten.
Slice the cucumber thinly.
Make the dressing by combining the vinegar, salt, pepper, sugar and oil and pour this mixture over the cucumber.
Sprinkle chopped dill and borage over the dressed cucumber.

Norwegian Porridge

Rømmegrøt
Norway

Many Norwegian dishes were devised a long time ago and, like this porridge, have been handed down from generation to generation. Pinhead or coarse oatmeal was the forerunner of bread, so it is not surprising that it is held in special esteem. Oatmeal porridge is served on many festive occasions, especially at country weddings, where it is customary to begin the wedding feast with the traditional *røm-megrøt*, sprinkled with sugar and cinnamon.

150 g (5 oz) coarse porridge oats,
1 litre (1 3/4 pints) water, 1/2 tsp salt

Boil the oats with the water and salt for 5 minutes and leave to swell. Stewed fruit, sour milk or fresh cream are all good accompaniments. Sultanas can also be cooked with the porridge or 2–3 tablespoons chopped nuts can be stirred in, thus producing a hearty meal which is rich in fibre.

Rose-hip Soup

Nyponsoppa
Sweden

Wild berries grow in profusion in the summer months in the forests and on the moorlands of Scandinavia. The Swedes are keen berry collectors. They use these delicious sweet-and-sour fruit to prepare appetizing soups or sauces as accompaniments for meat dishes. The small berries are also much loved as desserts, in cakes, made into fruit juices or in alcoholic preparations.
Rose-hips, in common with all other berries, have a high vitamin content. This sweet rose-hip soup is often served before a main course.

600 g (1 1/4 lb) rose-hips (cut in half, hairs and seeds scraped out of centres),
1.5 litres (2 1/2 pints) water, juice of 1 lemon, grated rind of 1/2 untreated lemon,
80–100 g (2 1/2–3 1/2 oz) sugar (according to taste and the sweetness of the fruit),
pinch of ground cinnamon or 1/2 cinnamon stick, pinch of salt, 2 1/2 tbsp cornflour, up to 125 ml (4 fl oz) white wine,
50 g (2 oz) ground almonds, 1 egg yolk, 15 g (1/2 oz) butter or 125 ml (4 fl oz) fresh cream (whipped)

Allow the rose-hips to soak in hot water for a few hours. Add the grated lemon rind and juice, sugar, cinnamon and salt, and cook until the berries are soft. Then purée the mixture. Mix it with cornflour and flavour with the white wine. Stir in the ground almonds and check the seasoning again. Thicken it with egg yolk. Finally, beat the butter into the purée or garnish it with the whipped cream. Rose-hip soup can be eaten cold or reheated, but it should not be allowed to boil again after the egg yolk, butter or cream are added. Macaroons or other biscuits go well with it.

Cockscomb Pastries

Hanekamme
Denmark

Cockscomb pastries are made from *wiener-brødsdej*, Danish puff pastry dough. This is just one of the many shapes into which these tempting Danish pastries are made.
A Danish housewife offers her family or invited guests, at least four different kinds of pastries – usually home-baked – with their afternoon coffee.

---

120 g (4 oz) almond paste (uncooked marzipan), 80 g (2 1/2 oz) apple purée, grated rind of 1/2 untreated lemon, 1/3 portion Danish Pastry Dough (see p. 19), 1 tbsp flour, 1 egg yolk to coat, coarse white sugar, 15 g (1/2 oz) butter for the baking sheet

---

Mix the marzipan with the apple purée and the lemon rind. Sprinkle a pastry board with flour and roll out the dough into a rectangle. Spread the marzipan and apple mixture over half the rectangle, lengthways. Fold the other half over it and press down firmly. Slice the filled pastry into 5–6 cm (2 inch) pieces and make 4–5 cuts in each piece. Brush with egg yolk and sprinkle with the coarse white sugar. Leave to rest for 15–20 minutes, then bake on a buttered baking sheet in a preheated oven at 180 °C (350 °F, gas mark 4) for about 20 minutes. Cool on wire racks.
Instead of using coarse sugar, the cockscomb pastries can be coated with a sugar glaze (a very thin icing) when they have cooled.

Lamb Stew with Cabbage

Får i kål
Norway

After fish, lamb is the mainstay of Norwegian cuisine. The land is too mountainous to permit any large-scale arable farming or animal husbandry. For centuries, sheep and goats have been the main livestock, though there are dairy cattle.
Får i kål is a nourishing meal, which is especially appreciated on cold days.

*1 kg (2–2 1/2 lb) lamb (shoulder, neck or leg),
1 white or Savoy cabbage (about 800 g–1 kg;
1 3/4–2 lb), 1 onion, salt,
10 black peppercorns in a muslin bag,
1 sprig thyme, 1 litre (1 3/4 pints) stock,
6 potatoes, 1/2 bunch parsley (chopped)*

Slice the meat into large cubes. Quarter the cabbage, discard the stem and wash, blanch and shred it finely. Chop the onion.
Place the cabbage and meat in alternate layers in a casserole with a tight-fitting lid. Add the thyme, salt and peppercorns. Pour the stock over the mixture, cover and cook on low heat for about 1 hour. In the meantime, peel the potatoes, dice them and add to the pan. Cook for another 30 minutes. Remove the bag of peppercorns and the thyme. Serve sprinkled with the parsley.
It should be noted that this dish tastes even better after it has been reheated for the third time.

Swedish Hash

Pytt i panna
Sweden

In Sweden, potato dishes enjoy great popularity. We have the inventiveness of the Swedish housewife to thank for this nutritious *pytt i panna*, which roughly translated means "tidbits in the pan". It is a typical fried dish, simple and quick to make. The meat and potatoes can be precooked in separate pans, and then combined and served together. It is a very good way to use up meat leftovers from the previous day.

6 potatoes, 3 tbsp oil,
30 g (3/4 oz) butter, 3 onions,
400 g (14 oz) roast or boiled meat leftovers or
200 g (7 oz) raw or cooked ham,
salt, pepper, a few sprigs parsley (chopped),
4 eggs

Wash the potatoes and cut them into small equal-sized cubes. Pat dry with a cloth and fry them in the oil-and-butter mixture for 16–18 minutes, turning frequently, until they are golden-brown. Remove from the pan.
Brown the onions in the same fat until they are translucent. Cube the meat or ham to the same size as the potatoes and add it to the pan. Return the potatoes to the pan briefly and season with salt and pepper.
Arrange the hash on four plates and sprinkle chopped parsley over it. Place a fried egg in the centre of each helping. The traditional way to serve this dish is to add a raw egg yolk to each helping of hash, which can then be mixed in at the table. Beetroot or pickled gherkins go well with this dish.

Stuffed Pike

Täytetty hauki
Finland

There was no end to their hospitality! If I wanted to eat, I would have to catch the fish myself. All I was allowed for the main course was a fishing rod and some bait, my host informed me as we arrived at the small lake. The air was redolent with the aromas of early autumn and the forests gleamed with bright colours. I held a fishing rod for the first time in my life. Spellbound, I stared at the lake for minutes at a time. A movement down there in the water, a tug and I had a bite – it was a pike.

1 pike (about 1.5 kg/3 lb), 1 lemon, salt,
2 hard-boiled eggs, 1 bunch parsley,
50 g (2 oz) cooked brown rice,
freshly ground white pepper,
60 g (2 oz) butter (cut into small pieces),
1 tbsp dry breadcrumbs,
8 prunes (halved, stoned and soaked in water
for 2 hours), basic fish stock (optional),
lemon slices,
butter for greasing dish

Clean and gut the pike, but do not remove the head. Sprinkle lemon juice and salt over the inside and outside of the fish. Chop the eggs and parsley, reserving a few sprigs of parsley for the garnish. Add these ingredients to the rice and season with salt and pepper. Stir half the butter into the rice mixture together with the breadcrumbs. Stuff the fish with this mixture. Arrange the prunes over the stuffing. Sew up the fish. Butter a fireproof oven dish liberally and place the fish on it. Dot the fish with the rest of the butter and put in a preheated oven for about 1 hour at 180 °C (350 °F, gas mark 4). If you wish, pour some fish stock over the fish. Serve garnished with parsley and lemon segments.

Blueberry (Bilberry) Tart

Mustikkapiirakka
Finland

August is one of the most beautiful of the summer months in Finland. Now is the time for the crayfish feasts. Life seems to be lived mostly in the open air, in the woods and by the lakes and rivers.

August is also the time when the blueberries (bilberries) ripen. They are eagerly collected to make juice or jam. The berries can also be dried and eaten in dishes such as this bilberry tart.

For the pastry: 150 g (5 oz) butter,
150 g (5 oz) brown sugar, 2 eggs,
2 tsp baking powder,
100 g (3 1/2 oz) wholemeal flour,
100 g (3 1/2 oz) ground hazelnuts.
For the topping:
400 ml (14 fl oz) sour cream, 2 eggs,
80 g (2 1/2 oz) sugar, 1 sachet vanilla sugar,
grated rind of 1/2 untreated lemon,
1/2 tsp anise, 350 g (12 oz) blueberries
(bilberries)

To make the pastry: cream the butter and sugar. Beat in the eggs one at a time and continue to mix. Sift the flour and baking powder and add them to the mixture, then add the hazelnuts. Beat or knead until the mixture is smooth. Roll out the pastry to fit a circular buttered baking tin or shallow piedish about 23 cm/9 inches in diameter.

To make the topping: combine all the ingredients except the bilberries. Fold in the berries carefully and pour this over the pastry. Bake for about 35 minutes at 180–200°C (350–400°F, gas mark 4–6).

Herrings in Sherry

Sild i Sherry
Denmark

Immature herrings are known as Matjes herrings. They are not very large, but are tender and plump. From about June, they are caught and cleaned on board the fishing boats, then gutted, lightly-salted and stored in barrels. Matjes make an excellent *smørrebrød* delicacy. This first mouth-watering morsel is sometimes accompanied by icecold akvavit. When served with potatoes boiled in their skins and dotted with butter, Matjes are a light, delicious and economical dish.

4 Matjes herrings, 2 onions.
For the marinade:
5 tbsp vinegar, 6 tbsp water, 2 tsp sugar,
3 tbsp oil, 8 tbsp dry sherry, 4 allspice berries,
1 bay leaf.
Sprigs of dill

Rinse the Matjes herrings if necessary and fillet them. Slice the onions in rings and arrange them on top of the fillets.
To make the marinade: combine the vinegar, water, sugar, oil, sherry, allspice and bay leaf and pour this over the Matjes fillets. Leave in the refrigerator, at least overnight. Garnish with dill sprigs.
Coarse, thickly-buttered wholemeal bread and a glass of beer round off this treat.

Baltic Herring Bake

Silakkalaatikko
Finland

The Finns love strongly-flavoured dishes. Baltic Herring Bake therefore has a secure place in their cuisine. It is a very filling meal. A glass of beer goes particularly well with its salty taste.

---

4 washed and salted Baltic herrings,
800 g (1 3/4 lb) potatoes,
2 pickled cucumbers (thinly sliced),
200 g (7 oz) pork, 150 g (5 oz) lamb,
1 large onion (finely chopped), 3 tbsp oil,
up to 500 ml (16 fl oz) fresh cream,
2–3 eggs, 2 crushed allspice berries.
Butter for greasing the dish.

Bone the herrings and dice them. Peel the potatoes and slice them thinly. Dice the pork and lamb and brown the meat in the oil with the finely-chopped onion. Arrange the potato slices, herring, meat and pickled cucumbers in layers in a buttered fireproof dish. Whisk the eggs and cream, add the allspice and pour over the other ingredients. Cook in a preheated oven at 160°C (310°F, gas mark 2 1/2) for about 1 1/2 hours.

"Uli" Herring Gratin

Sillgratin "Uli"
Sweden

The Swedes esteem herring *sill*, above all other fish. The idea that it is more than just another food to eat, is clear from the fact that a distinction is made between herring and other fish. It is amazing how many delicious recipes Swedish cooks, both professional and amateur, can devise based on herring. "Uli" herring gratin is suitable for any occasion or time of day.

300 g (10 oz) floury boiled potatoes,
300 g (10 oz) apples (preferably Russets or
Cox's Orange Pippins),
juice of 1/2 lemon, 2 onions,
1 tbsp butter, 8 herring half-fillets,
generous 250 ml (8 fl oz) fresh cream,
250 ml (8 fl oz) crème fraîche,
a dash of pepper

Peel the potatoes and the apples. Core the apples and slice them, sprinkling them immediately with the lemon juice, to avoid discolouration. Slice the onions and potatoes so finely that they are practically translucent. Carefully layer the potatoes, apples, well-washed herring fillets and onions in a buttered, fireproof soufflé dish. Combine the cream, crème fraîche and pepper and pour the mixture over the layers. Place in a preheated oven and bake for about 35 minutes at 180 °C (350 °F, gas mark 4). It is also a good idea to make the Gratin in individual gratin dishes, in which case the cooking time is reduced to 15 minutes.

Herring Salad and Glassblower's Herring

Sillsallad och Glasmästarsill
Sweden

These herring dishes are always on the table for any smörgåsbord.

Herring salad for 4–6 persons: 3 Matjes or salt herrings, 200 g (7 oz) salted tongue, 4 potatoes boiled in their skins, 3 cooked pickled beetroot, 2 apples, 2 pickled cucumbers, 1–2 onions, 1 bunch dill, yolks of 4 hard-boiled eggs, 1 tsp mustard, 2 tbsp white wine vinegar, 2 tbsp oil, 125 ml (4 fl oz) sour cream, 125 ml (4 fl oz) fresh cream, 3 tbsp beetroot juice, salt, pepper

Rinse and fillet the herrings, dice them. Dice the tongue, potatoes, beetroot, apples and pickled cucumbers. Chop the onion and dill. Pass the egg yolk through a sieve and mix with the mustard. Add the rest of the ingredients, pouring the liquids over the salad and carefully stirring them in. Leave to stand, lightly covered in a cool place until well chilled.

Glassblower's herring: 4 salt herrings, 250 ml (8 fl oz) wine vinegar, 250 ml (8 fl oz) water, 1/2 cup sugar, 4 red onions, 1 carrot, 2 bay leaves, 1 piece fresh ginger root, 1 piece fresh horse-radish, 2 tsp mustard seeds, 6 whole allspice berries, a little coriander

Fillet the salt herring and soak overnight. Boil the vinegar, water and sugar for about 20 minutes, then leave to cool. Thinly slice the onions and carrot. Slice the herring into 2–3 cm (1 inch) thick strips and layer with the vegetables, herbs and spices in a bowl. Pour on enough marinade to barely cover the herrings. Cover tightly with a lid or cling film and leave to marinate in the refrigerator for 2–3 days.

Lobster Ragoût

Hummerstuvning
Sweden

The lobster is related to the crayfish. Those caught in the North Sea and the Atlantic can be as heavy as 750 g (1 1/2 lbs). It mainly populates the coastal waters near mussel beds, where it finds a well-stocked larder. Its tender and delicious flesh has always been very popular. Our lobster ragoût ranks as a particularly impressive starter.

1 uncooked lobster, salt, pinch of sugar,
2 tbsp vinegar, 1 onion (finely chopped),
1 carrot, 5 peppercorns, 50 g (2 oz) butter,
1 spring onion (finely chopped),
30 g (1 oz) flour, 125 ml (4 fl oz) fish stock,
125 ml (4 fl oz) fresh cream,
freshly ground white pepper,
few drops of Worcester sauce,
1 egg yolk, 1 bunch dill,
40 g (1 1/2 oz) grated cheese

Scrub and rinse the lobster. Half-fill a large pan with water, add the salt, sugar, vinegar, finely-chopped onion, carrot and peppercorns, and bring to the boil. Plunge the lobster head first into the water. Leave for about 20–25 minutes. After it has cooled, remove it from the stock and split lengthways. Remove the flesh from the shell and slice it into strips. Melt the butter and sauté the spring onion in it. Stir the flour into the butter and beat until smooth. Stir in the fish stock and the cream. Season and leave to simmer for a few minutes. Add the lobster meat, beat in the egg yolk, add some chopped dill and place the mixture in little buttered dishes, scallop shells or pastry cases. Sprinkle with the grated cheese and place in a preheated oven at 180 °C (350 °F, gas mark 4) to bake for a few minutes. Garnish with sprigs of dill before serving.

Jansson's Temptation

Janssons Frestelse
Sweden

This piquant recipe with the promising name of Jansson's Temptation is one of the most typical Swedish dishes. No-one really knows the origins of the name. One story is that it was invented by an opera singer called Pelle Janzon about one hundred years ago; he wanted to offer his friends something to stimulate their thirst. Others attribute the name to a bishop named Janson. In any case, neither name is spelled like the name of the recipe. Today this dish is so popular that it is found on every *smörgåsbord*.

In Sweden, the recipe always calls for anchovies, but these are not the very salty anchovy fillets imported into the rest of Europe from Portugal or North Africa, but young, lightly-salted Baltic herring.

6 potatoes, 3 onions, 3 tbsp butter,
15 Swedish anchovy fillets,
400 g (14 oz) fresh cream, pepper,
2–3 sprigs dill, a few chunks of lemon

Peel the potatoes and slice them into matchstick-thin strips. Slice the onions thinly and sauté in two-thirds of the butter until golden. Use the rest of the butter to grease a fireproof dish and layer it alternately with potatoes, onions and anchovy fillets, ending with a layer of potatoes. Season the cream with pepper, add the freshly chopped dill and pour it over the mixture. The potatoes should be covered by the cream. Bake for about 50 minutes in a preheated oven at 180 °C (350 °F, gas mark 4). Garnish with lemon chunks and serve in the dish.

Boiled Cod with Mustard Sauce

Kokt torsk med sennepsaus
Norway

When one speaks about the Norwegian fishing industry, one cannot help thinking of the Lofoten Islands. From January to April, thousands of boats put to sea to catch the North Atlantic cod. The younger fish, the Baltic cod, known as torsk, is particularly good to eat, because it is low in calories and high in protein. Hung over a wood fire and dried in the open air, it is called *torrfisk* or *stokkfisk*. When it is gutted, split open, salted and dried on the cliffs *(klippen)*, it is called *klippfisk*.

*1 kg (2–2 1/2 lb) North Atlantic cod,
2 tbsp lemon juice, salt, 750 ml (1 1/4 pints)
water, 1 bay leaf, 4 peppercorns.*
For the sauce:
*30 g (1 oz) butter, 20 g (3/4 oz) flour,
3 tsp medium-strong mustard, 250 ml (8 fl oz)
fish stock, 250 ml (8 fl oz) fresh cream,
pepper, pinch of sugar.
1 lemon, few sprigs dill*

Sprinkle the cleaned cod with lemon juice, season with salt and cut each fish into 4 steaks. Bring the water to the boil with the salt, bay leaf and peppercorns. Reduce the heat and add the cod slices. Leave for 10–12 minutes to simmer according to the size of the cod, but do not allow to boil. Remove the cod carefully with a slotted spoon and keep warm.

To make the sauce: melt the butter, and stir in the flour to make a roux. Add the mustard and stir in the fish stock. Add the cream, allow to cook for a while and season.

Arrange the fish on a large dish with chunks of lemon and dill sprigs. Serve the sauce separately. Rice or parsleyed potatoes and a fresh salad go well with this fish dish.

Cod au Gratin

Torskgratin
Norway

For thousands of years, fish has been one of the mainstays of the Norwegian diet. According to legend, the abundance of fish in the seas around Norway was so great in former times that one only needed to dip one's hand in the water to grab a plump catch!
Even today, fish are still plentiful. The most important fish for the Norwegians has always been North Atlantic cod. Its firm white flesh is much prized and can be prepared in many delicious and different ways.

---

800 g (1 3/4 lb) North Atlantic cod fillet,
juice of 1/2 lemon, salt, 2 onions,
120 g (4 oz) celeriac, 250 g (8 oz) carrots,
1 leek, 60 g (2 oz) butter,
125 ml (4 fl oz) stock,
125 ml (4 fl oz) fresh cream, pepper,
1 bunch parsley, 2 tbsp breadcrumbs,
2 tbsp grated cheese,
2 tbsp butter cut into small pieces

Rinse the cod fillet under running water, pat dry, season with salt and sprinkle with lemon juice. Chop the onions. Dice the vegetables and sauté them in the butter. Stir in the stock and cream and leave to simmer for 10 minutes. Season with salt and pepper. Arrange the vegetables in a fireproof dish. Place the fish on top and sprinkle with chopped parsley. Then top with the breadcrumbs and grated cheese and dot the surface with small pieces of butter. Bake in a preheated oven at 180°C (350°F, gas mark 4) for 30–35 minutes.

Caramelised Potatoes

Sukkerbrunede kartofler
Denmark

The Danes love caramelised vegetables. Caramelised potatoes and browned cabbage accompany many different dishes. For example, roast goose stuffed with apples and prunes is always served with two kinds of potato dish, sautéed and boiled. Try these caramelised potatoes for yourself. You will be surprised how good they taste.

800 g (1 3/4 lb) small potatoes (all about the same size), 45 g (1 1/2 oz) sugar, 70 g (2 1/2 oz) salted butter

Wash the potatoes thoroughly. Boil them in their skins, allow to cool and peel. Let the sugar slowly caramelise in a frying-pan over low heat. The sugar should only be allowed to brown lightly; if it gets too dark it will taste bitter. Add the butter and brown the potatoes all over until they are a rich golden-brown.

Potato and Carrot Soufflé

Peruna-porkkana-laatikko
Finland

he Finns call their equivalent of the Swedish
nörgåsbord, voileipäpöytä. They can boast
uite a wide range of ingredients. Apart from
eat, game, fish, vegetables and bread, there
 a wide variety of potato dishes, including
ufflés.

750 g (1 1/2 lb) potatoes,
250 g (1/2 lb) carrots,
3 eggs, 30 g (1 oz) butter,
125 ml (4 fl oz) fresh cream, salt,
pinch of sugar, white pepper, nutmeg,
3 tbsp chopped parsley,
fat for the dish,
breadcrumbs,
30 g (1 oz) small pieces of butter

ook and purée the potatoes and carrots.
eparate the eggs. Cream the butter with the
gg yolks and add to the purée together with
he cream. Season and add the parsley. Whip
he egg whites until stiff and fold into the
ixture. Place in a greased fireproof dish.
prinkle with breadcrumbs and dot with the
mall pieces of butter. Bake in a preheated
ven at 175 °C (325–350 °F, gas mark 3–4)
or 50–60 minutes.

Stuffed Potato Dumplings

Kroppkakor
Sweden

Potatoes are the most popular of all vegetables in Sweden and one of the main staple foods. In many households, they are served in different forms as often as twice a day. This very tasty variation illustrates just what a Swedish cook is able to create from potatoes.

1 kg (2–2 1/2 lb) potatoes,
60 g (2 oz) potato flour (farina),
20 g (3/4 oz) flour, 1 egg, 1 egg yolk,
salt, pepper, pinch of nutmeg.
For the filling: *125 g (4 oz) smoked streaky*
bacon (rind removed), 1 large onion,
100 g (3 1/2 oz) mushrooms, 1 tbsp oil,
a few stalks of parsley, salt, pepper.
Melted butter to pour over the dumplings

If possible, wash and boil the potatoes in their skins the previous night. The next day, mash the peeled potatoes and knead with the potato flour, flour, whole egg, egg yolk and seasoning. **To make the filling**: dice the bacon, onion and mushrooms and sauté them in the oil. Add the chopped parsley, and season with a little salt and pepper.

Knead the potato mixture until smooth and roll it out into a long rectangle about 2 cm (1/2 inch) thick. Slice it into 12 pieces of the same size. Place some filling in the centre of each of the pieces of potato dough and shape into balls, so the filling is firmly enclosed.

Bring a large pan of salted water to the boil. Reduce the heat until the water simmers. Use a slotted spoon to carefully lower the dumplings into the water and cook for 10–12 minutes. Do not let the water come back to the boil. Remove the dumplings from the water and pour melted butter over them. They are often served with lingonberries or cranberries.

Grated Potato Pancake and Potato Salad

Rårakor med gräslök och Potatissallad
Sweden

The high regard that the Swedes have for the potato, is shown by the enormous price that new potatoes can command in spring and by the overwhelming opinion that potatoes are the basis for every Swedish meal.

Grated potato pancake:
6 potatoes (peeled), salt, pepper, 1 bunch chives, 1 onion, 4 tbsp oil, 2 tbsp butter

Grate the peeled potatoes on a coarse grater and season with salt and pepper. Drain off any liquid. Cut the chives finely, finely chop or grate the onion and mix them into the potato. Heat the oil and add the butter. Meanwhile, make small flattened pancakes using 2 tbsp of the grated potato per pancake. Fry for about 3 minutes on each side until brown and crisp.
A fresh salad is a good accompaniment.

Potato salad:
8 potatoes cooked in their skins, 1 onion, 2 pickled beetroots, 2 cucumbers pickled in vinegar, 4 herring fillets, 1 bunch chives, 1/2 bunch parsley, 2 1/2 tbsp vinegar, salt, pepper, 8 tbsp oil

Peel the potatoes and slice them. Chop the onion and dice the beetroot, cucumbers and herring fillets. Chop the herbs finely and add them to the mixture. Stir the vinegar, salt, pepper and the oil thoroughly together and pour this over the salad. Leave for 1 hour until the potatoes are quite cold and have absorbed the flavours.

Norwegian Potato Rissoles

Potetkaker
Norway

There is no doubt that fish dishes occupy first place in Norway but, the Norwegians are also very fond of potatoes. One of their savoury specialities is potato rissoles. When eaten with a crisp salad, they make an excellent meal which is very quick to prepare and serve. If any rissoles are left over, they can be served cold the next day. They will still taste just as delicious.

400 g (14 oz) potatoes, salt,
120 g (4 oz) dry breadcrumbs,
125 ml (4 fl oz) fresh cream, 1 egg,
2 tbsp chopped parsley,
2 tbsp grated cheese,
125 g (4 oz) lean diced ham,
pepper, nutmeg, oil for frying

Peel the potatoes, cook them for about 20 minutes in salted water and then push through a sieve. Mix two-thirds of the bread-crumbs with the cream, egg, parsley and cheese. Add the ham cubes, then mix this with the potatoes, and season to taste. Shape the mixture into round patties about 6–8 cm (2 1/2–3 inches) in diameter. Roll the patties in the rest of the breadcrumbs and fry them in the hot oil until golden.

Cheese Salad and Cheese Soufflé

Ostesalat og Ostesoufflé
Denmark

Denmark's intensive dairy-farming makes it the main producer of cheese in Scandinavia.

Cheese Salad: 250 g (8 oz) Havarti cheese, 1/2 cucumber, 250 g (8 oz) cooked ham, 2 cooking apples, 2 tbsp mayonnaise, 2 tbsp fresh cream, 2 tbsp yogurt or sour cream, salt, pepper, pinch of grated horseradish or curry powder, a few lettuce leaves

Peel the cucumber, peel and core the apples and dice them with the cheese and ham. Combine the mayonnaise, cream and yogurt. Season and add the horseradish or curry powder. Pour the liquid over the salad ingredients and leave to soak for 1 hour in the refrigerator. Arrange salad on lettuce.

Cheese Soufflé: 40 g (1 1/2 oz) butter, 35 g (1 1/4 oz) flour, 125 ml (4 fl oz) milk, 250 ml (8 fl oz) fresh cream, 160 g (5 1/2 oz) grated cheese, salt, pepper, nutmeg, 4 eggs (separated), 2 tsp cornflour, butter for greasing the dish

Melt the butter, add the flour and make a roux. Gradually pour in the milk and cream, stirring constantly. Stir in the grated cheese. Season with salt, pepper and nutmeg. Remove from the stove and leave to cool a little. Mix the cornflour with the egg yolks and stir into the sauce. Whip three of the egg whites into stiff peaks and fold them into the mixture. Pour the mixture into a buttered fireproof dish and bake in a preheated oven at 190–200°C (375–400°F, gas mark 5 1/2–6) for about an hour. If baked in ramekins, this cheese soufflé makes a good starter. In this case, reduce the baking time to 20 minutes.

Kissel and Rhubarb and Strawberry Kissel

Kiisseli ja Raparperimansikka-kiisseli
Finland

The Finns have always been very close to nature and are happy to prepare their food from what nature has to offer. Kissel is a dessert made from the thickened juice of soft fruits, especially berries.

Kissel: Sugar (according to taste and the sweetness of the fruit juices), 750 ml (1 1/4 pints) berry juice, 3 tbsp cornflour or potato flour (farina), 4 tbsp water, juice of 1/2 lemon, 200 g (7 oz) fresh soft fruit (optional), 250 ml (8 fl oz) fresh cream

Bring the juice and sugar to the boil. Mix the cornflour with the water and add to the juice. Bring to the boil then remove from the stove immediately. Add the lemon juice and fresh fruit, if desired. Chill in the refrigerator until very cold. Serve with lightly whipped cream.

Rhubarb and Strawberry Kissel: 400 g (14 oz) rhubarb, 250 ml (8 fl oz) water, about 100 g (3 1/2 oz) sugar, 1/2 vanilla pod, 2 tbsp cornflour, 4 tbsp water, 250 g (8 oz) strawberries, 250 ml (8 fl oz) fresh cream

Wash the rhubarb well and remove the leaves and any tough skin. Slice the stalks into 2–3 cm (1 inch) chunks. Cook for about 15 minutes in the water with the sugar and the vanilla pod. Discard the vanilla pod. Combine the cornflour with water and stir into the rhubarb. Bring to the boil, reduce the heat and simmer gently for 3 minutes, then leave to cool. When cold, stir in the halved strawberries. Chill and serve with whipped cream.

Danish Doughnuts

Æbleskiver
Denmark

The Danes call these delicacies *æbleskiver*. Neither apple-slices nor doughnuts is an accurate translation of what is really meant. Perhaps this delicious pastry was called by this name because it used to be cut open and filled with apple jelly. Æbleskiver are served with afternoon or evening coffee.

For about 30 doughnuts:
4 eggs (separated), 30 g (1 oz) sugar,
250 g (8 oz) flour, 40 g (1 1/2 oz) yeast,
about 250 ml (8 fl oz) tepid milk,
200 ml (7 fl oz) fresh cream,
grated rind of 1 untreated lemon,
pinch of salt, ground cardamom,
50 g (2 oz) butter, cooking fat for frying,
icing sugar, apple jelly or brandy-flavoured
chocolate sauce

Cream the egg yolks with the sugar. Add the flour and cream. Dissolve the yeast in the warm milk and add it to the mixture. Flavour with lemon rind, salt and cardamom. Add the melted butter, mix well. Whip 3 of the egg whites into stiff peaks and fold them into the mixture. Leave to stand, covered, for 1 hour. In Denmark, a special pan with 7 or 9 hollows is used for cooking these doughnuts. Warm the pan on the stove, brush it with the cooking fat and pour some of the mixture into each of the hollows. As the doughnuts expand, only half-fill the hollows. As soon as the underside is golden-brown, turn the doughnuts over with a knitting needle and cook the other side. The doughnuts will emerge as round balls. Serve them hot, sprinkled with icing sugar and accompanied by apple jelly. As an alternative, a brandy-flavoured chocolate sauce is also very good with this.

Boiled Crayfish

Keitetyt ravut
Finland

In Sweden, as in Finland, people celebrate enthusiastically and as often as possible. In August, there are traditional crayfish banquets in both countries. Where possible these feasts are held in the open air and plenty of the boiled, red, succulent crayfish are consumed.

In Finland, they are eaten accompanied by toast, beer and vodka. The Swedes prefer to drink Akvavit.

8 live crayfish per person,
5 litres (9 pints) water,
450g (1 lb) salt,
2 tbsp dill seeds,
2 dill crowns,
3 bunches dill

Scrub the crayfish clean with a brush. Bring water to the boil with the salt, dill seeds, dill umbels and dill and lower the crayfish gently, one by one, into the rapidly boiling water. Cover and return the water to the boil. Cook for another 8 minutes. Leave the crayfish to cool in the liquid. Arrange them decoratively on a dish or platter. Strain a little of the cooking liquid, pour it over them and garnish with the bunches of dill and dill crowns.

Poached Salmon with Fish Potatoes

Dampet laks
Denmark

Salmon is known worldwide as a luxury. Whether this has to do with the fact that it can only be caught in a few areas or because of its especially delicious flavour is not clear. In any case, this noble fish also has an important place on the Danish menu. Above all, it is an essential ingredient in the festivals which occur throughout the year. The more simply it is prepared, the more it retains its genuine flavour. Fish potatoes are excellent with this variation.

1 small salmon (about 1.5 kg/3 lb; gutted and descaled, left whole),
salt, 3 bunches dill, 1 glass dry white wine.
For the fish potatoes:
1.2 kg (2 1/2 lb) small oval-shaped potatoes,

Marinated Salmon

Gravad lax
Sweden

In this recipe, the salmon is buried for two or three days under the salt, sugar and dill. This gives it an exceedingly delicate flavour and the flesh is so tender that the slices virtually melt on the tongue.

For 8 people:
1.5 kg (3 lb) salmon (middle cut),
2 tbsp coarse salt,
1 tbsp white peppercorns, (coarsely ground),
1 1/2 tbsp sugar, 2 bunches fresh dill,
1–2 lemons

Scale and gut the salmon, and slice it in half lengthways. Remove the backbone and all the other bones. Combine the salt, coarsely-ground peppercorns and sugar. Lay one half of the salmon, skin side down, in a casserole. Sprinkle the salt mixture over it and cover with the washed dill. Lay the second half of the fish, skin side up, over the first one. Cover with aluminium foil. Place a wooden board over it and weigh it down with weights (you can use heavy cans of preserves for this purpose). Leave in the refrigerator for 2–3 days. During this time, turn the salmon several times and baste it, on the underside as well, with the juices which it has exuded. Always cover it again well afterwards. To serve, remove the herbs, pat the salmon dry and slice it diagonally against the grain into thin slices. Arrange on a platter and garnish with small bouquets of dill and lemon slices. As a main dish, the salmon should be accompanied by a mustard sauce, white bread or dill potatoes as well as a cucumber salad.

For a smørrebrød: Serve the salmon on a slice of white bread with chopped cucumber, garnished with a sprig of dill and a slice of lemon. Mustard sauce is served on the side.

Lamb in Dill Sauce

Kokt lamm med dillsås
Sweden

It is typical of Scandinavian cuisine to enhance even meat dishes with dill sauces and garnish them with dill sprigs. Dill seems to be an indispensable herb of which abundant use is made.

1 litre (1 3/4 pints) water,
1.2 kg (2 1/2 lb) lamb (shoulder or breast),
1 bouquet garni (dill, parsley, bay leaf),
4 white peppercorns, 2 cloves,
1 carrot, 1 onion, 1 piece celeriac,
40 g (1 1/2 oz) butter, 30 g (1 oz) flour,
salt, pepper, pinch of sugar,
1/2 tsp mild mustard, 1 tbsp lemon juice,
1 tsp vinegar, 4 tbsp chopped dill,
1 egg yolk, 125 ml (4 fl oz) sour cream,
a few sprigs dill to garnish, 1 lemon

Bring the water to the boil. Put in the lamb and skim off the scum which forms on the surface of the water. Add the bouquet garni, peppercorns and cloves together with the chopped vegetables. Cook for about 1 1/2 hours at a low temperature. Remove the lamb, keep it warm in aluminium foil and strain the stock through a sieve.
Melt the butter, stir in the flour and make a roux. Whisking constantly with an egg whisk, gradually beat in 500 ml (16 fl oz) of the lamb stock. Bring to the boil and let it barely simmer for 10 minutes. Add the herbs and seasoning. Mix the egg yolk and sour cream with half a cup of the sauce. Remove the pan from the heat and stir the egg yolk mixture into it. Taste, and adjust the seasoning if necessary. Place the lamb on a serving dish and pour the sauce over it. Garnish with dill and chunks of lemon.
New potatoes, rice or noodles are an ideal accompaniment.

Liver Pâté

Leverpostej
Denmark

Liver pâté is a basic ingredient in the Danish cold buffet, the *kolde bord*, and is even eaten at breakfast. It is also popular as a spread for *smørrebrød*, Danish open sandwiches.

2 onions, 2 tbsp oil, 650 g (1 1/2 lb) liver,
300 g (10 oz) green (unsmoked) bacon,
60 g (2 oz) anchovy fillets,
30 g (1 oz) butter, 2 tbsp oil,
2 tbsp breadcrumbs,
250 ml (8 fl oz) fresh cream, 3 eggs,
salt, pepper, ground allspice, nutmeg,
pinch of ground cloves, 1/2 tbsp thyme,
1/2 tbsp marjoram, Madeira wine,
350–400 g (12–14 oz) smoked bacon rashers
(rinds removed) for lining the terrine

Sauté the chopped onions in the oil until translucent, and leave to cool. Feed the liver, bacon, anchovy fillets and onion twice through the finest setting of a mincing machine. Mix the butter well with the flour, breadcrumbs and cream and add to the minced liver mixture. Fold in the eggs one by one. Stir the mixture thoroughly, because this improves the quality of the pâté. Add the herbs and spices, season to taste. Line a terrine or a loaf tin with bacon slices and put the mixture into it. Cover with aluminium foil and place in a water bath in the centre of a pre-heated oven for about 1 1/2–2 hours at 180 °C (350 °F, gas mark 4). Do not turn out until the pâté is completely cold. The pâté is often served with gherkins and beetroot, but it is also suitable as a starter.

To use it on a *smørrebrød*, take a slice of wholemeal wheat-and-rye bread, lay a lettuce leaf on it, then a slice of liver pâté, then some sautéed mushrooms. Top with onion rings and tomato segments and garnish with sprigs of parsley.

Mackerel

Makrell
Norway

After herring and cod, the mackerel features prominently in the Norwegian menu. Its juicy aromatic flesh makes it suitable for grilling, but it can also be steamed, baked, fried or smoked. Mackerel is not only popular because of its flavour, but also because it can be used in many different ways.

2 mackerel (about 500 g; 1 lb) each,
juice of 1/2 lemon, salt.
For the sauce:
2 onions (finely chopped), 50 g (2 oz) butter,
2 tbsp flour, 1 tsp curry powder,
1/2 tbsp chopped ginger, 2 apples,
1 tbsp lemon juice, 375 ml (12 fl oz) chicken
stock, 125 ml (4 fl oz) fresh cream,
a little thyme, salt,
1 tbsp mango chutney (optional)

Gut and wash the mackerel, sprinkle them with lemon juice and season with salt. Cook them in a fish-kettle or steamer for 15–20 minutes.

To make the sauce: sauté the finely chopped onions in the butter until translucent. Add the flour, curry powder and ginger. Grate the apples, sprinkle them with lemon juice and add them to the onions. Stir in the chicken stock and cream. Thyme, salt and mango chutney (if desired) complete the sauce, which is served with the mackerel.

Mashed potatoes are a good accompaniment.

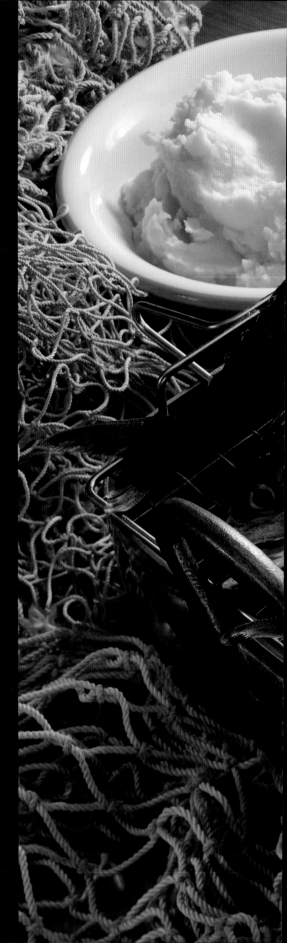

National Day Dessert

Grundlovsdessert
Denmark

King Frederick IX signed a new Constitution on 5th June 1953, whereby Denmark officially changed from a constitutional monarchy into a democratic parliamentary one. Since then, this day has been celebrated as National Day. What could be closer to the Danish heart than the creation of a delicious sweet called "National Day Dessert"?

600g (1 1/4 lb) rhubarb, about
125g (4 oz) sugar, 2 tbsp lemon juice,
250ml (8 fl oz) milk,
1 vanilla pod (split and scraped),
3 leaves red gelatine and 3 leaves white
gelatine, 4 eggs (separated),
250ml (8 fl oz) fresh cream,
30g (1 oz) slivered almonds

Remove any stringy skin and leaves from the rhubarb, and slice the stalks into 2–3-cm (1-inch) pieces. Put in a pan with 250ml (8 fl oz) water, the lemon juice and half of the sugar and bring to the boil. Reduce the heat and simmer for 15 minutes Bring the milk to the boil with the vanilla pod. Simmer for a few minutes, then remove from the heat and leave to cool a little. Discard the vanilla pod. Soak the gelatine leaves in a cupful of water until soft and discard surplus water and dissolve the soaked, squeezed gelatine leaves in the milk. Cream the egg yolks with the rest of the sugar, add the vanilla-flavoured milk and leave to cool. As soon as the milk mixture begins to thicken, whip the egg whites into stiff peaks and fold them into the mixture with half the whipped cream.
Pour the rhubarb into individual glass bowls and cover with the thickened milk mixture. Sprinkle with the slivered almonds and serve with the remaining whipped cream.

Easter Cheese Dessert

Pasha
Finland

Pasha is a Karelian Easter speciality eaten as a dessert or with coffee. Traditionally wooden moulds carved with Christian symbols were used. Today a clean earthenware flowerpot lined with muslin gives the shape and allows the whey to drain.

*1 kg (2–2 1/2 lb) curd cheese,
200 g (7 oz) butter, 3 egg yolks, 1 whole egg,
150 g (5 oz) sugar, 200 ml (7 fl oz) fresh
cream, 1 vanilla pod (split and scraped),
50 g (2 oz) candied lemon peel (finely
chopped), 50 g (2 oz) candied orange peel
(finely chopped), 50 g (2 oz) almonds,
50 g (2 oz) sultanas soaked in Suomuurain
(cloudberry liqueur) or other fruit liqueur,
1/2 tbsp cloves, 1/2 tbsp cinnamon,
1–2 tbsp lemon juice, 15–20 whole almonds,
glacé cherries*

Press the curd cheese in a cheesecloth to squeeze out the liquid. Melt the butter and combine it with the cheese. Cream the egg yolks and whole egg with the sugar. Beat in the cream gradually and add the vanilla pod. Put the bowl in a double-boiler over gentle heat and stir the mixture until it has the consistency of a thick cream. Remove it from the heat and continue stirring until it has cooled, then fold it into the curd cheese. Add the candied peels, almonds, sultanas, cloves, cinnamon, and the lemon juice. Line a new 1.5-litre (2–1/2 pint) earthenware flowerpot with a piece of dampened muslin or cheesecloth, and spoon the mixture into it. The cloth should be large enough to be folded loosely over the top of the mixture. Place a weight on the pot and stand it in a cool place. Leave for 1 to 2 days, then turn out the Pasha and decorate it with the almonds and glacé cherries.

Pancakes

Plättar
Sweden

There are two kinds of egg pancakes in Sweden. The large ones, cooked in an ordinary frying-pan, are called *pannkaka*. The small ones, known as *plättar*, are cooked several at a time in a special pan. If you don't own a Swedish *plättpanna*, you can use any other small frying-pan instead. The same batter is used for both kinds of pancake. These thin, crêpe-like egg pancakes can be filled with meat or vegetables, but they can also be served for dessert with fruit, wild berry compote or jam.
The Swedes like to eat this dessert after the traditional Thursday pea soup.

For 4–6 persons:
3 eggs, up to 250 ml (8 fl oz) single cream,
75 g (2 1/2 oz) flour,
40 g (1 1/2 oz) melted butter,
a pinch of salt, a pinch of sugar,
1 sachet vanilla sugar.
Melted butter for frying

Beat the eggs well with half the liquid. Gradually add the flour, beating constantly until the mixture is smooth. Add the rest of the liquid, melted butter, salt, sugar and vanilla sugar. Stir well and leave to stand for 15 minutes. Put the pancake pan on the stove and brush it thoroughly but sparingly with melted butter. Put 1 tablespoon of batter per pancake in the pan. Depending on the size of the pan, you could cook several at a time. Cook each pancake for 1–2 minutes on either side until crisp and golden.

Parsonage Dessert

Pappilan hätävara
Finland

The Finns probably gave this dessert its name because the parsonage is known to help the needy. In this recipe it is a case of helping the housewife. If an unexpected guest turns up, she can quickly improvise a delicious dessert from leftover cake or biscuits. Cream and berries are always readily to hand in Finland.

250 ml (8 fl oz) fresh cream,
500 g (1 lb) blackberries, 1 tbsp sugar,
pinch of cinnamon,
pinch of ground cloves,
sponge fingers or leftover cake or biscuits,
extra berries and cream for garnish

Whip the cream. Add the washed berries, sugar, cinnamon and ground cloves. Arrange alternate layers of sponge and the fruit-and-cream mixture in dessert bowls. Leave in a cool place for the flavours to mingle. To serve, decorate with berries and cream.

144

Wild Mushrooms in Cream Sauce

Sienimuhennos
Finland

Every summer and autumn, the vast forests of Finland yield a rich harvest of edible mushrooms which the Finns use to enliven their diet. The nature-conscious Finns are not only enthusiastic berry gatherers, but they are also outstandingly knowledgeable about mushrooms. The oldest way to preserve wild mushrooms is to dry them. This is the best way to preserve their true flavour, and it also means that delicious mushroom dishes can be prepared outside the mushroom season.

---

600 g (1 1/4 lb) fresh mushrooms (ceps, chanterelles, field mushrooms or a mixture), 1 tbsp lemon juice, 1 onion, 40 g (1 1/4 oz) butter, 1–2 tbsp flour, a generous 250 ml (8 fl oz) fresh cream, salt, freshly ground white pepper, finely chopped herbs (parsley, chives, dill, chervil, lovage), 125 ml (4 fl oz) sour cream

---

Clean and wash the mushrooms, cut them into small pieces and sprinkle them with lemon juice. Dice the onion and sauté it in the butter. Add the mushrooms and, after 5 minutes, sprinkle with the flour and stir in the fresh cream. Cook gently for a few minutes. Season with salt and pepper. Add the herbs and complete the sauce with the sour cream.

Potatoes, rice, pasta or bread are all good accompaniments.

Boiled Salt Brisket

Oxbringa
Sweden

Skåne is Sweden's breadbasket. Herds of beef cattle graze in the lush green meadows. Orchards, kitchen-gardens and flower gardens complete this colourful picture and give the impression of a land flowing with milk and honey.

2 kg (4 lb) salted brisket of beef, 1 leek,
1 carrot, 1 piece celeriac, 1 Hamburg parsley
root (padrushka), parsley.
For the horseradish sauce:
40 g (1 1/2 oz) flour, 40 g (1 1/2 oz) butter,
500 ml (16 fl oz) stock,
50 g (2 oz) currants or sultanas,
salt, pinch of sugar, 1 tbsp lemon juice,
1 tsp freshly-grated horseradish or to taste

Rinse the brisket thoroughly to remove excess salt. Place it in boiling water. Reduce the heat and simmer for about 10 minutes, then start skimming the surface. Wash the vegetables, tie them into a bundle and add them to the water after half an hour of cooking. Continue to simmer for another 1 1/2 hours. In the meantime, make the horseradish sauce.

To make the horseradish sauce: stir the flour into the melted butter to make a roux. Gradually stir in the stock and simmer for 8–10 minutes. Add the currants and remove from the heat. Add the salt, sugar, lemon juice and the horseradish, stirring constantly.

Slice the brisket and arrange it on a serving platter. Pass round the horseradish sauce separately. Carrots cooked in the stock, potatoes with cream or parsleyed new potatoes are ideal accompaniments.

For a *smørrebrød*: boiled salt brisket can be served in an open sandwich on pumpernickel bread with horseradish sauce and paper-thin slices of carrot, garnished with a sprig of parsley.

Partridges Stuffed with Ceps

Rapphöna
Sweden

The partridge is the most sought-after of all the game birds, because of its fine flavour. It lives in coveys in meadows and on moorlands. Young partridges which can be recognized by their yellow legs and sharp dark beaks, have particularly tender flesh and are therefore favourites.

1 onion, 80 g (2 1/2 oz) butter,
200 g (7 oz) ceps, salt,
freshly-ground white pepper,
1 bunch parsley, 2–3 tbsp breadcrumbs,
4 young partridges,
200 g (7 oz) bacon rashers (rinds removed),
250 ml (8 fl oz) stock, 250 ml (8 fl oz) fresh
cream, 2 tbsp cornflour, Madeira,
1 truffle (optional)

Sauté the chopped onion in 20 g (3/4 oz) of the butter in a sauté pan until translucent. Clean the ceps and chop them into small pieces; add them to the onion in the pan. Season with salt and a little pepper and cook until the mushrooms are soft. Stir in the chopped parsley and the flour and leave to cool. Stuff the prepared partridges with the mixture, sew them up and wrap them in the slices of bacon. Fry the partridges on both sides, breast side down first, in the remaining butter. When they are lightly browned all over, stir in the stock and cover the pan. Cook for about 50 minutes, depending on the size of the partridges, basting frequently. Thicken the sauce with cream and cornflour, flavour with Madeira and season with salt and pepper. A few thin slices of truffle added to the sauce increases the pleasure.

Braised Haunch of Venison

Rådyrlår
Norway

The game found in the mountainous regions of Norway has been much prized in the native cuisine since time immemorial. It offers a welcome addition to the menu, which otherwise consists mainly of saltwater fish.

1 haunch of venison (about 2.5 kg/5 lb),
200g (7 oz) bacon sliced into thin strips,
salt, freshly ground white pepper,
1 large slice bacon fat, fat for frying,
1 carrot, 1 onion, 150g (5 oz) celeriac,
1 Hamburg parsley root (padrushka),
1 bunch parsley, thyme, 1 bay leaf,
2 allspice berries, 5 juniper berries,
500ml (16 fl oz) milk,
125ml (4 fl oz) fresh cream,
250ml (8 fl oz) sour cream

Wash the venison haunch and pat it dry, then lard it with the bacon strips. Rub the meat with salt and pepper and cover it with the bacon fat. Heat the cooking fat in a large, ovenproof casserole with a tight-fitting lid and brown the meat all over. Add the chopped vegetables, as well as the herbs and seasoning. Pour the milk over the meat and cover the pot. Place it in the oven, preheated to 190 °C (375 °F, gas mark 5). Braise for 2 1/2 hours. Remove the venison and keep it hot. Strain the cooking liquid and transfer it to a saucepan. Boil it for 5 minutes, then remove it from the heat. Stir the fresh and sour cream into the liquid and check the seasoning again. Mushrooms and cranberries are very popular accompaniments to this dish. Goat's cheese added to the cream sauce also complements the meat well.

Rice Pudding

Risgryngröt
Sweden

Swedish families today still spend their Christmas in accordance with the old traditions. They celebrate in a large family gathering to which good friends are also invited. There is dancing round the decorated Christmas tree holding hands and Christmas carols are sung. Then the festive meal begins.
Rice pudding, sprinkled with cinnamon and sugar, is never missing from a Swedish Christmas menu.

Generous 750 ml (1 1/4 pints) milk,
1 vanilla pod (split and scraped),
pinch of salt,
160 g (5 1/2 oz) short-grain rice (rinsed),
1 blanched almond,
100 g (3 1/2 oz) butter cut into small pieces,
80–100 g (2 1/2–3 1/2 oz) sugar,
2 tbsp ground cinnamon

Add the vanilla pod and salt to the milk and bring to the boil. Add the rinsed rice, return the liquid to a brisk boil, then cover and cook over a low heat until the rice is soft and swollen. Remove the vanilla pod and stir in the almond. Pass round butter and the sugar-and-cinnamon mixture separately.

Nowadays, some people like to vary the recipe by stirring chopped almonds and sultanas into the cooled rice, folding in whipped cream, flavouring with kirsch liqueur and adding 1 or 2 cloves when cooking.

The cooked rice can also be flavoured with cinnamon, a beaten egg added and the mixture put into a buttered soufflé dish, dotted with butter and baked in a preheated oven for 10 minutes at 180–200 °C (350–400 °F, gas mark 4–6). A kirsch or rose-hip sauce goes very well with this.

Reindeer Steak

Poronlihapihvi
Finland

The *Same* or Lapps are a nomadic people who inhabit the northern regions of Scandinavia. Their most important possessions are their large reindeer herds, which they continuously drive to new pastures. The reindeer provides the *Same* with practically everything they need to survive. Reindeer meat may be hard to find, if you cannot get it, use venison instead.

4 reindeer steaks, salt,
freshly ground white pepper, 1 tbsp flour,
2 tbsp oil, 1 tbsp butter, 1 glass red wine,
100 ml (3 1/2 fl oz) game stock,
1 tsp lemon juice,
100 ml (3 1/2 fl oz) fresh cream

Salt and pepper the steaks and dust them lightly with flour. Heat the oil, add the butter and fry the steaks on both sides. Remove them from the pan and keep them warm. Deglaze the frying juices with red wine. Stir in the stock and cook briefly to make a sauce. Add the lemon juice and cream and check the seasoning.
Morels, berries and a Scandinavian version of roast potatoes are good accompaniments. These latter are potatoes cut into half-moon shapes with blunt ends, that are browned on the stove and then roasted in the oven to finish cooking. They are served with parsley.

Beef Scouse

Brun Lapskaus
Norway

Lapskaus is an old seafarer's recipe and is known in various forms in all the ports visited regularly by Scandinavian seamen, from Lübeck to Liverpool. The ingredients not only lend this dish flavour, but also guarantee a hearty meal, which no doubt appealed to the seafarers of long ago.

4 slices rump steak weighing about
160–180 g (5–6 oz) each,
salt, freshly ground white pepper,
2 onions, 2 carrots, 50 g (2 oz) butter,
1 tbsp flour, 1–2 tsp mustard,
generous 500 ml (16 fl oz) meat stock

Salt and pepper the steaks. Slice the onions and carrots into rings. Melt the butter in a frying-pan and fry the steak on both sides. Add the onions and cook them until they are translucent, then add the carrots. Dust with the flour, season with mustard and stir in the stock. Cover and simmer for 35 minutes over a low heat, until the meat slices are tender. Savoy cabbage and potatoes cooked in stock are an ideal accompaniment.

Beef Broth with Dumplings

Köttsoppa med klimp
Sweden

The Swedish housewife sometimes provides a hearty meat-and-vegetable soup to keep her family warm in the winter. This is one example.

400 g (14 oz) beef brisket or silverside,
1.5 litres (2 1/2 pints) water,
1 piece celeriac (chopped), 1 leek (sliced),
2 carrots (sliced),
1 Hamburg parsley root (padrushka),
salt, pepper, 2 drops Worcester sauce,
125 ml (4 fl oz) fresh cream, 1 tbsp butter,
60–80 g (2– 2 1/2 oz) flour,
20 g (3/4 oz) semolina, 2 eggs,
nutmeg, 1/2 bunch parsley

Put the beef into the cold water, add the vegetables and bring to the boil. Simmer for a good hour, until the meat is cooked through and tender. Remove the meat and reserve it. Season the cooking liquid with salt and pepper.

In a separate saucepan, combine the cream and butter. Stir the flour and semolina into the fat and cook, stirring constantly with a wooden spoon, until the mixture comes away from the bottom of the pan in one lump. Remove from the heat, allow to cool a little and gradually stir in the eggs. Season with salt and nutmeg. Stir in the chopped parsley. Use a teaspoon to scoop out small balls of dough and shape them into dumplings. Drop the dumplings into the boiling broth. Leave to cook for about 10 minutes. Cut the meat into small pieces and return it to the soup.

Stuffed Meat Roll

Rullepølse
Denmark

Rullepølse is a very spicy speciality of the Danes. It is ideal as an ordinary sandwich filling, but it is also popular as a component of *smørrebrød* on a more festive occasion.

300 g (10 oz) boneless lean pork,
300 g (10 oz) beef, salt,
reshly ground black pepper, allspice,
ground cloves, 1 onion,
2 tbsp chopped parsley, 1 tbsp lovage,
1 boned pork loin roast (about 1 kg–2 1/2 lb).
For the brine:
1.25 litres (2 pints) water, 250 g (8 oz) salt,
2 tsp saltpetre, 2 1/2 tbsp sugar

Slice the lean pork into thin strips, season it and combine it with the chopped onion, parsley and lovage. Lay the pork loin out flat on a board and spread the mixture over it. Roll up the loin into a sausage shape and tie securely with string.

To make the brine: bring the water to the boil, add the salt, saltpetre and sugar, stir and remove from the heat. Leave to cool until cold.

Lay the rolled pork in the liquid, ensuring that it is completely covered by the brine, and let it steep for 3 days in a cool place. The pork roll should then be cooked for 1 1/2 hours in stock or water. Remove it from the water and place it under a weighted board to press out any excess liquid. When it has cooled completely, remove the string, slice it and serve with rye bread and home-pickled gherkins.

To make a *smørrebrød*: lay a slice of the meat roll on rye bread and garnish it with rings of onion and sweet red pepper.

Pickled Beetroot

Krydrete rødbeter
Norway

This popular vegetable, which originates from
the Mediterranean, has been cultivated since
the Middle Ages. It is a robust plant which
is an ideal crop for the short Norwegian
summer. In common with all root vegetables,
beetroot is rich in minerals and for this reason
it is very healthy. It can be prepared in numerous ways. Beetroot is popular in salads and
soups because it adds both colour and
flavour. Pickled beetroot is always provided in
the Norwegian cold buffet, the *koldbord*.

---

1 kg (2–2 1/2 lb) beetroot, 7 tbsp vinegar.
For the marinade:
125 ml (4 fl oz) water, 2 tbsp sugar, salt,
freshly ground black pepper, 1 bay leaf,
2 cloves, 1/2 tsp caraway seeds,
2 small slices horseradish (optional).
6 tbsp oil, 1 onion

Scrub the beetroot thoroughly until clean. Be
careful not to cut the roots or skin before
cooking, or the red colour will drain out.
Pour 1 1/2–2 litres (2 1/2–3 1/2 pints) water
into a deep pot, add half the vinegar and bring
to the boil. Add the beetroot and simmer for
about 50 minutes. Leave to cool until luke-
warm.
Meanwhile make the marinade. Briefly boil
the rest of the vinegar with the marinade
ingredients.
Peel the tepid beetroot or remove the skin by
hand, cut into thin slices and place in a bowl.
Add the oil and the chopped onion to the
marinade ingredients, mix well and pour the
liquid over the beetroot. Cover and leave in a
cool place for 12–14 hours, stirring occasionally.

Red Cabbage

Rødkål
Denmark

The Danes eat a lot of cabbage in winter. Red cabbage is a good accompaniment for roast goose or duck, but it also goes well with roast pork. The addition of blackcurrant juice adds a piquant flavour and enhances the colour of the red cabbage. It is amazing what the Danes can manage to produce from this vegetable. It is even occasionally used raw to garnish a *smørrebrød*, or used as the basis for a delicious salad.

1 red cabbage (about 1 kg/2 lb), 1 onion,
2 apples, 1 tbsp lemon juice,
50 g (2 oz) butter, 125 ml (4 fl oz) water,
3 tbsp vinegar,
125 ml (4 fl oz) blackcurrant juice or jelly,
2 cloves, 1 tbsp sugar,
salt, a little allspice

Remove the outer leaves of the cabbage. Cut the head into quarters, remove the stalk and slice or shred the cabbage. Chop the onion, peel and core the apples and cut them into thin slices. Sprinkle them with the lemon juice. Melt the butter. Briefly sauté the onion and apple and add the red cabbage. Pour in the water, vinegar and blackcurrant juice, add the seasonings and simmer gently for about 1 1/4 hours over low heat. Check seasoning again before serving.

Cream Sauce with Goat's Cheese

Fløtesaus med geitost
Norway

Goats and sheep thrive in Norway's mountainous landscape, and also contribute to the local diet.
The hard, brown goat's cheese known in Norwegian as *geitost* has a strong flavour and creamy texture. It is served sliced on thin crispbreads. Its strong aroma makes it particularly suitable for flavouring sauces.

30 g (1 oz) butter, 20 g (3/4 oz) flour,
generous 125 ml (4 fl oz) roasting juices or
stock, 125 ml (4 fl oz) fresh cream,
2 tsp redcurrant jelly,
30 g (1 oz) Norwegian goat's cheese (geitost)
or other goat's cheese (sliced),
125 ml (4 fl oz) sour cream,
salt, freshly ground white pepper

Melt the butter in a saucepan and add the flour to make a roux. Stir in the cooking juices or stock, add the cream and cook gently, stirring constantly, for 8–10 minutes. Add the redcurrant jelly and the sliced goat's cheese and stir over a low heat until the cheese melts. Remove the sauce from the heat. Quickly stir the sour cream into it and season with salt and pepper to taste.

Roast Pork with Crackling

Flæskesteg med svær
Denmark

For this roast you need a cut from back or a piece from the middle loin, leaving the rind on.

For 12–14 persons:
1 boned pork joint (about 2 kg/5 lb), salt, black pepper, English mustard powder, 10–12 cloves, 2 bay leaves.
For the sauce: *about 500 ml (16 fl oz) stock, 500 ml (16 fl oz) fresh cream, salt, pepper, 2 tbsp tomato purée, 1 tbsp cornflour*

Score the pork rind with cuts in a diamond pattern, and season well with salt and pepper. Rub the rind with mustard powder and stick the cloves and bay leaves into the rind. Lay the meat on the oven rack with the rind uppermost. Allow the fat to collect in a pan. Roast for about 4 hours in an oven preheated to 150–160°C (300–325°F, gas mark 2–3). Sprinkle the roast with cold water for the last 20 minutes and raise the temperature to 210°C (400–425°F, gas mark 6–7). Leave the meat to rest a while before carving.
To make the sauce: skim the fat from the cooking juices, stir the stock and cream, simmer gently for 10 minutes. Season with salt, pepper and tomato purée. For a thicker sauce, mix the cornflour with a tablespoon of the liquid and stir into the sauce.
Serve with red cabbage, caramelised potatoes, home-made cranberry sauce, gherkin pickled with mustard seeds and cornichons.
To make a *smørrebrød*: arrange a slice of roast ham on rye bread and coat with remoulade sauce. Garnish with cucumber sliced in a fan-shape and red cabbage salad.

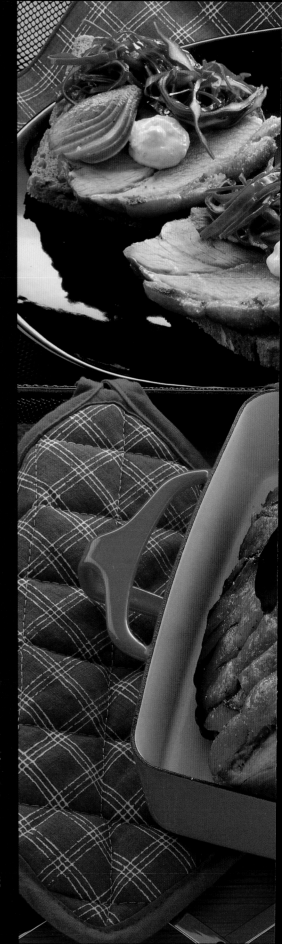

Sloe Gin

Oratuomi-snapsi
Finland

Finns still have a special relationship with nature and make full use of the rich gifts of the immense forests and lakes. In autumn, they roam the forests, collecting the different kinds of wild berries. Cloudberries, *lakka*, *mesimarja*, the arctic raspberry, *karpalo* and *puolukka*, two kinds of cranberry, grow throughout the country and are popular as accompaniments for game dishes.

The blue-black fruits of the blackthorn bush are collected after the first frost. They are tart but aromatic, are rich in vitamins and their juices are drunk fresh or made into liqueurs. The Finns often use these wild fruit to add to their own form of schnapps.

1 1/2 cups (about 375 g/12 oz) sloe berries,
2 tsp honey, about 500 ml (16 fl oz) 40% pure
schnapps or gin

Wash the sloes, dry them carefully, and put them in the freezing compartment of the refrigerator. When frozen, bottle them. Add the honey and fill the bottle to the top with schnapps or gin. Seal well. Leave for 3–4 months, after which time you will have a wonderfully aromatic sloe gin.

Chimneysweep

Sotare
Sweden

This is one of the most delicious ways to cook the small Baltic herring. It is grilled over the hot embers of a wood fire, either in the open air or in the hearth, which is why this dish is called Chimneysweep. If you do not have a grill, you can cook the herring in a frying-pan, as suggested here, but cooking it on a naked flame will give the fish the characteristically smoky taste which makes Chimneysweep so delicious.

---

1 kg (2–2 1/2 lb) fresh small Baltic herring, salt, 5 tbsp oil, 2 tbsp butter.
For the sauce:
1 bunch dill, 1/2 bunch parsley, 1 bunch chives, 1–2 tsp capers, 125 ml (4 fl oz) fresh cream, 125 ml (4 fl oz) sour cream, salt, freshly ground white pepper

---

Gut the herrings, discard the heads and fins, wash thoroughly and pat dry. Rub the fish with salt. Heat the oil in a large cast-iron frying-pan and add the butter. Fry the herring for 7–10 minutes (according to size) on both sides until crisp and golden-brown. Keep hot until all the fish are done.

To make the sauce: chop the dill and parsley and finely chop the chives and capers. Mix the fresh and sour cream with half of the herbs. Season with salt, pepper and capers.

Sprinkle the rest of the herbs over the fish and serve the cream sauce separately. Boiled potatoes go very well with this dish.

Swedish Salad

Svensk sallad
Sweden

More than half of Sweden is covered by forest. Only about one-tenth of the total land mass is cultivated, but the farming is intensive. The fertile lands of southern Sweden provide the most important agricultural products. Thanks to the surrounding sea and the numerous inland lakes and waterways, fishing also has a special significance. Some of the riches of the earth and the sea come together in Swedish salads.

200 g (7 oz) boiled beef,
200 g (7 oz) boiled potatoes,
200 g (7 oz) cooked beetroot,
1 sour apple, 2 pickled cucumbers,
1 buckling.
For the sauce:
2 tbsp vinegar, salt, freshly ground
white pepper, 1 tsp mustard, pinch of sugar,
6 tbsp oil.
1 tbsp capers, fresh herbs (parsley, dill,
chives), 2 hard-boiled eggs (quartered)

Cut the beef, potatoes, beetroot, apple and pickled cucumbers into cubes. Gut the buckling, remove the bones and use a fork to break the fish into small pieces.

To make the sauce: combine the vinegar, salt, pepper, mustard and oil and pour over the salad.

Mix in the capers and chopped herbs. Garnish with egg segments and dill sprigs. Refrigerate and serve chilled.

Pork with Apples and Potatoes

Svinermørbrad med æbler og kartofler
Denmark

This dish is eaten often and with great relish in Denmark. Danish food is also the richest in the whole of Scandinavia.

Danes love their food. It is not unusual for Danes to eat five or six small meals a day. *Smørrebrød*, the Danish open sandwich, is very popular as a snack between meals or a light meal on its own. Although the main meal of the day, at which the whole family gathers, is served in the evening, it is called *middag*.

800 g (1 3/4 lb) boneless neck end of pork,
3 tbsp oil, salt, freshly ground white pepper,
3 onions (sliced), 4 apples (sliced),
1 litre (1 3/4 pints) stock,
6–8 black peppercorns,
6 mustard seeds, 2 bay leaves,
1 kg (2–2 1/2 lb) potatoes (peeled and sliced)

Divide the pork into 4 equal-sized pieces and braise them all over in the hot oil in a flame-proof casserole. Season with salt and pepper. Add the sliced onion and the apple. Cook for about 10 minutes, then add the stock. Add the peppercorns, mustard seeds and bay leaf. Cover the casserole with a tight-fitting lid and transfer it to an oven preheated to 180 °C (350 °F, gas mark 4). Cook for about 50 minutes in all, adding the sliced potatoes after 30 minutes.

Pork Loin with Apples and Prunes

Luumuilla täytetty possupaisti
Finland

Pork loin with apples and prunes is a tasty and filling dish which goes extremely well with a glass of beer. At the end of the meal, berry liqueur and coffee are served. Any food left over can be served cold the next day.

1.5 kg (3 lb) neck end of pork (boned and rolled), 160 g (5 oz) prunes, 2 apples, salt, freshly ground white pepper, pinch of cloves, pinch of rosemary, 35 g (1 oz) butterfat (a mixture of butter and lard), 250 ml (8 fl oz) stock, 125 ml (4 fl oz) sour cream

Make a cut along the length of the joint of meat or get this done by the butcher. Soak the prunes in water or cold tea for 1 hour, stone them leaving the liquid. Peel, core and dice apples and mix them with the prunes, reserving a few prunes for the sauce. Stuff the pocket in the joint with apple-and-prune mixture. Skewer or sew up the pocket. Rub the joint with herbs and spices and brown it all over. Pour the stock over it, cover and cook in a preheated oven at 180 °C (350 °F, gas mark 4) for about 1 1/4 hours. Simmer the remaining prunes in the soaking liquid. Remove the roast from the oven, transfer it to a serving dish and keep it warm. Make a sauce by pouring the liquid from the cooked prunes into the casserole and heat gently. Let it simmer, add the sour cream and check the seasoning. Serve the sauce and the prunes with the meat.

Sailor's Beef

Sjömansbiff
Sweden

In the early 16th century a fleet of warships was built in the Stockholm shipyards, under the direction of King Gustavus Vasa. This reinforced Sweden's political position as a great power. The merchant fleet also benefitted from this progress and contested the right of the Hanseatic League to trade in the Baltic Sea area. Today, one is able to marvel at the sight of a royal warship built during this period. The ship, the *Vasa*, capsized immediately after it was launched in 1628, but was raised intact in 1961.

This recipe is many centuries old and was invented by sailors for their own consumption. It is doubtful whether it was quite so rich in former times, though beef must have been the main ingredient.

600 g (1 1/4 lb) beef (rump or silverside),
3 tbsp oil, 1 tbsp butter, salt, pepper,
3 onions sliced into rings,
cooking fat for greasing the dish,
700 g (1 1/2 lb) potatoes (peeled and thinly
sliced), generous 500 ml (16 fl oz) beer
fresh herbs (parsley, basil, lovage)

Cut the meat into large pieces. Heat the oil, add the butter, and brown the meat, then season with salt and pepper. Add the onion rings. Butter a fireproof dish and arrange the thinly-sliced potatoes in it. Lay the meat and onion rings on top and cover with more potato slices. Season again with salt and pour the beer over the stew. Cover, and cook in a preheated oven for about 1 hour at 200 °C (400 °F, gas mark 6).
Serve sprinkled with the fresh herbs.

Open Sandwiches

Smørrebrød
Denmark

Smørrebrød, the Danish open sandwich, is Denmark's great contribution to gastronomy. Here are some examples:

Glassblower's Herring (see p. 100) with red onion rings and pickled cucumber slices and lettuce on a slice of rye bread

Black bread with thin apple slices and Matjes herring fillet, topped with onion rings and dill sprigs

Smoked salmon with dill sprigs and horse-radish sauce on white bread

Rye bread with lettuce, buckling fillet and scrambled egg, garnished with fresh cucumber slices and dill

Danish crabs topped with a dollop of mayonnaise, and garnished with watercress and a lemon slice, arranged on white bread

Avocado slices and crab in cocktail sauce on wheat-and-rye bread, decorated with a slice of lemon

Cooked mussels on lettuce with watercress, radish rosettes and slices of lemon on dark rye bread

Smoked eel on black bread with scrambled egg and coarsely chopped chives

Slice of wholemeal bread with lettuce, fried fillet of plaice, a remoulade sauce and slice of lemon

Red and black caviar on slices of hard-boiled egg, garnished with lemon and arranged on toasted white bread on a bed of lettuce

Open Sandwiches

Smørrebrød
Denmark

Smørrebrød, the Danish open sandwich, consists of combinations of fish, crustaceans, and shellfish, meat, vegetables, salads, fruit and cheese elegantly arranged on slices of bread.

A thin slice of roast pork rolled into a cone-shape and filled with herring salad (see p. 100), garnished with sprigs of parsley and served on a slice of dark rye or wheat and rye bread

Slices of cooked turkey breast and melon arranged in a fan-shape on white bread, topped with black grapes

A slice of rye bread garnished with steak tartare and a raw egg yolk presented in a half-shell, surrounded by little mounds of finely-chopped onion, capers, pickled cucumber and beetroot

Asparagus tips rolled in a slice of cooked ham, garnished with remoulade sauce and watercress on mixed grain bread

Roast pork and crackling with apple slices and prunes on a piece of rye bread spread with lard

Slice of crispbread with air-dried ham, celeriac salad and a slice of tomato

Fried Danish camembert on wholewheat bread with cranberry sauce

Danish blue cheese on walnut bread with melon balls and black grapes

Cottage cheese on toasted white bread with fruit salad. The fruit salad can also be served in a separate dish

Spandau Pastries

Spandauer
Denmark

Nobody knows why these pastries are called Spandauer. Isn't it enough to say that they are a mouth-watering variety of Danish pastry? The cakes and pastries of Copenhagen are often given fanciful names. For instance, there are *skrubber og kamme*, scrubbing-brushes and combs, *æblekamme eller hanekamme*, applecombs or cockscombs, and *trekanter*, triangles.

1/3 portion Danish pastry dough (see p. 19),
3 tbsp raspberry jam or 3 tbsp redcurrant jelly,
confectioner's custard, slivered almonds
or chopped nuts, 1 egg yolk beaten with
1 tsp water for glazing, 15 g (1/2 oz) butter,
1 tbsp flour, cooking chocolate (optional)

Roll out the dough into a rectangle and slice it into squares of about 10–12 cm (4–5 inches). Put a teaspoon of jam or confectioner's custard into the middle of the dough square. Fold the corners into the middle and press down firmly. Sprinkle with the slivered almonds or chopped nuts. Brush the dough all over with egg yolk.

Lightly butter one or more baking sheets, depending on the size, sprinkle with a little flour and arrange the dough squares, leaving plenty of room between them. Leave to rise for 15 minutes. Bake in a preheated oven at 180–200 °C (350–400 °F, gas mark 4–6) for about 20–25 minutes until golden-brown.

Melted cooking chocolate can be dribbled over the cooled pastries.

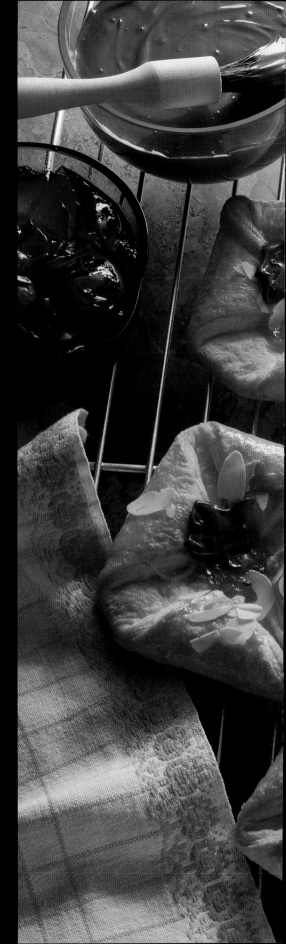

Swede Soup

Lanttusoppa
Finland

The Finnish climate restricts the variety of fresh vegetables available. On the other hand, Finnish cuisine offers an abundant choice of fish and meat dishes.

The swede declined in popularity, but it never completely disappeared from the Finnish menu, and it is again featuring as an ingredient in Finnish food.

---

1 onion, 1/2 swede, 3 tbsp butter,
2 tbsp flour, 1 litre (1 3/4 pints) meat stock,
salt, freshly ground white pepper,
nutmeg, 250 ml (8 fl oz) fresh cream,
1 bunch parsley, 4 tbsp grated cheese

Dice the onion and swede. Melt the butter in a saucepan and add the onion and swede. Sprinkle with flour and sweat the vegetables on a low heat for 5 minutes. Stir in the meat stock. Season with salt, pepper and nutmeg and simmer for about 25 minutes. Before serving, stir in the cream, chopped parsley and grated cheese and taste for seasoning.

Veiled Peasant Girl and Lemon Cream

Bondepige med slør og Citronfromage
Denmark

Danish girls don't actually wear veils, but perhaps the whipped cream reminds one of a veil under which something sweet is concealed.

Veiled Peasant Girl: 60 g (2 oz) butter, 50 g (2 oz) brown sugar, 250 g (8 oz) grated rye bread, 50 g (2 oz) grated chocolate, 250 g (8 oz) apple purée, 100 g (4 oz) raspberry jam or 250 g (8 oz) fresh raspberries, a little vanilla sugar, 250 ml (8 fl oz) fresh cream, chocolate shavings for decoration

Melt the butter in a saucepan and fry the sugar and grated rye bread, stirring continuously. Cool a little, then mix with the grated chocolate. Arrange alternate layers of the breadcrumb mixture, apple puree and raspberries or raspberry jam in a glass bowl, ending with a layer of breadcrumbs. Leave to cool thoroughly. Whip the cream with the vanilla sugar and spoon it over the pudding. Sprinkle with chocolate shavings.

Lemon Cream: 4 eggs (separated), 150 g (5 oz) icing sugar, grated rind of 1 untreated lemon, juice of 3 lemons, 4 leaves gelatine, 125 ml (4 fl oz) apple juice, 125 ml (8 fl oz) fresh whipped cream

Cream the egg yolks and icing sugar. Add the grated lemon rind and lemon juice. Soak the gelatine in cold water and squeeze out excess water. Heat the apple juice to below boiling point and dissolve the gelatine in it. Leave to cool, then add it to the cream mixture. Beat the egg whites into stiff peaks and fold them into the mixture with half the whipped cream. Chill for 1 hour. Decorate with the rest of the whipped cream before serving.

Cream Waffles and Crispy Waffles

Vafler/Våfflor
Norway/Sweden

Cream waffles are a Norwegian speciality. They taste wonderful with afternoon coffee. The Swedes prefer crispy waffles.

To make about 8 cream waffles:
*80 g (2 3/4 oz) butter, 1 tbsp sugar,
1 vanilla pod, 2 eggs (separated),
160 g (5 1/2 oz) sifted flour,
250 ml (8 fl oz) sour cream,
pinch of salt*

Cream the butter, sugar, the scraped out vanilla from the pod, and egg yolks. Add the sifted flour, sour cream and a pinch of salt. Whip the egg whites until stiff enough for a knife cut to leave a clear mark, then fold them into the butter mixture. Heat a waffle iron, greasing it if necessary, then put a little of the mixture in the centre of the iron. Close the lid and cook for a few minutes. Serve the waffles sprinkled with icing sugar, or hand round some jam.

To make about 8 crispy waffles:
*125 ml (4 fl oz) cold water,
160 g (5 1/2 oz) flour,
60 g (2 oz) melted butter,
200 ml (7 fl oz) whipping cream,
2 tsp sugar, 1 vanilla pod*

Stir the water into the flour. Stir in the cooled melted butter, whip the cream and add it. Add the sugar and scrape out the insides of the vanilla pod and add it to the mixture. Cook the waffles in a preheated waffle iron. Serve with jam or fruit and whipped cream.

Christmas Ham

Julskinka
Sweden

Scandinavia, Christmas is celebrated on
hristmas Eve. The Christmas Eve meal is as
uch a highlight of the festival as the beauti-
lly decorated tree with its burning candles.
lightly salted Christmas ham is part of this
adition. It is often served with red cabbage
nd apple sauce. As the centrepiece of the
nörgåsbord, it is served cold on a platter,
it in half and garnished with oranges and
apes.

To serve about 10 people:
1 cured ham (about 3–4 kg/6 1/2–9 lb),
1–2 bay leaves, 3 cloves, 4 peppercorns,
1 1/2 tbsp medium mustard,
1 tsp ground allspice, 1 egg, 1 tsp sugar,
dry breadcrumbs

---

eave the ham to soak in water overnight. Put
ie bay leaves, cloves and peppercorns into
bout 4 litres (7 pints) fresh water and bring
o the boil. Lay the ham in the water and add
nough extra water to just cover the ham.
ook for 3 1/2–4 hours, depending on the
ize of the ham. Beat the egg, mustard and
llspice together. Cut away the rind, and
rush the ham with the egg mixture. Combine
he sugar and breadcrumbs and cover the ham
ompletely with the mixture, pressing it in
ightly. Place the ham on a trivet in a roasting
in in an oven preheated to 200 °C (400 °F,
;as mark 6), and roast until the crust is golden
nd crisp.

Browned White Cabbage Soup

Brynt vitkålsoppa
Sweden

Genuine Swedish cuisine is called *husmans-kost*, or plain fare. This robust white cabbage soup is one of the most popular of the cabbage dishes eaten during the cold months of the year. Thanks to its peasant origins, it is simple and nourishing. Nowadays, many Swedes are returning to these traditional dishes of their ancestors.

1 kg (2 lb) white cabbage, 1 onion,
40 g (1 1/2 oz) butter, 1 tbsp brown sugar,
1.5 litres (2 1/2 pints) meat stock,
1 ham bone, salt, pepper,
1 tsp caraway seeds,
4 sausages (optional)

Discard the outer leaves of the white cabbage. Divide the head into quarters, cut out and discard the stalk, then shred the cabbage. Sauté the chopped onion in the butter. Add the shredded cabbage, and let it brown a little. Add the sugar, then stir in the stock. Add the ham bone and caraway seeds, cover, and cook on low heat for about 40 minutes. If you wish, sausages can be added to cook for a few minutes before serving.

Stuffed Onion Balls

Lökdolmar
Sweden

Since Scandinavian winters are so long, it is important to stock up with fresh vegetables that have good keeping qualities. Much use is therefore made of those that can be stored, such as brassicas and root vegetables. Onions are rich in vitamins and minerals.

For 4–6 persons:
2–3 large onions, each weighing
200–250g (7–8 oz)
For the filling:
1 finely-chopped onion, 20g (3/4 oz) butter,
1 boiled potato, 3 tbsp breadcrumbs,
300g (10 oz) lean minced beef,
2 tbsp fresh cream, white pepper, salt,
a few drops Worcester sauce (optional),
1 egg, 2 small bunches chopped parsley.
40g (1 1/2 oz) butter,
30g (1 oz) dry breadcrumbs

Peel the onions and poach them in water that is just below the boil for 40–45 minutes. Leave them to cool.
To make the filling: sauté the chopped onions in the butter until soft and translucent. Add the mashed potato and the other ingredients and mix together. Separate the poached onions into separate skins, and fill each skin with a little stuffing. Fold the ends over, and lay each stuffed ball, folded ends downwards, in a buttered fireproof dish. Melt the butter and pour it over the onion balls. Sprinkle with the breadcrumbs and bake for about 20 minutes in a preheated oven at 200°C (400°F, gas mark 6). The breadcrumbs should be crisp and golden.
These stuffed onion balls can be served as a starter, as part of a *smorgåsbord* or, in larger quantities, with mashed potatoes as a main course.

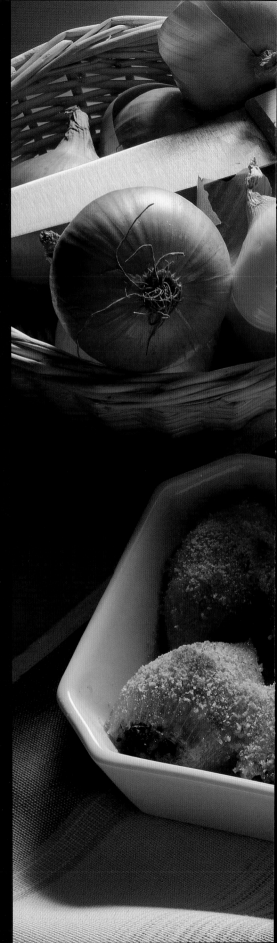

Recipes by Type of Dish

Unless otherwise indicated, the quantities given in the recipes are for four people. Liquid metric measurements are normally counted in decilitres in Scandinavia. In this book they have been given in millilitres. 1 dl = 100 ml, 1 litre = 10 dl, 1 litre = 1,000 ml.

Desserts, Porridge, Cakes, and Drinks

Alphabetical Index

Recipes by Country

Finland

Picture Credits